'THE GOUROCK'

"'THE GOUROCK'"

GEORGE "BLAKE"

THE GOUROCK ROPEWORK CO. LTD.

Port Glasgow, Scotland

Established
1736

December 1963

PRINTED BY PILLANS AND WILSON LTD. GLASGOW AND EDINBURGH

CONTENTS

ACKNOWLEDGEMENTS

.ees-Pedlar, Gourock
, Esq., A.M.I.P.A.
W. V. Kelly, Esq., Burgh Surveyor, Gourock
Mrs J. Rundell, S.S.I.
Commander H. E. Semple, R.N. (Retd.)
Aero-Pictorial Ltd., Boreham Wood, Herts
James Hall (Photographers) Ltd., Greenock
British Nylon Spinners Ltd.
Linen Industry Research Association
Shell Photographers Ltd., London
V. G. Miller, Esq., Manila, Philippines
The Birkmyre Canvas Co. (Pty.) Ltd., Sydney
Studio Swain, Glasgow
John Fullarton Birkmyre, Esq.
Radio Times Hulton Picture Library, London
Gourock Ropes & Canvas (Africa) Ltd., Johannesburg
British Geon Ltd., London
Ford Jenkins, Photographer, Lowestoft
A. A. Pomoell, Esq., Helsingfors, Finland
Gourock Ropes & Canvas Ltd., Buenos Aires
Gourock-Bridport Ltd., Montreal
Beken & Sons Ltd., Cowes, Isle of Wight
John A. Long, Esq., Bristol
Bertram Mills Circus Ltd.
Henry Birkmyre Semple, Esq.
Karsh of Ottawa

Acknowledgement is also due to the large number of staff and workers
of The Gourock Ropework Co. Ltd.—some now retired, some dead—
who provided so many views of early Port Glasgow from which the
reproductions used have been drawn.

FOREWORD

I am delighted that this book has at last been completed, as I have always been afraid that a lot of the colourful, unique and, at times, romantic history of our firm might have been lost.

You will see in this book how the Company started as separate entities in Gourock and in Port Glasgow. Both these concerns were very small until the time when they merged and the Birkmyre family came into the management. Later, when the Birkmyres had complete control they expanded the business from two very small local factories to an organisation which deals with cordage and canvas all over the world.

This, then, is as much the history of the Birkmyres as of The Gourock—as our Company is probably more generally known—for the names Gourock and Birkmyre are now quite synonymous. In fact, it would be true to say that the name 'Birkmyre' is better known throughout the world than the name 'Gourock'.

This book will also explain the anomaly of a firm with its Head Office in Port Glasgow but with its name taken from a small town seven miles away, and why some of our visitors, when visiting us, go to Gourock, expecting the factory to be there.

The factory and village of New Lanark are owned by The Gourock and there is also great interest in them and in the methods employed by Robert Owen, who was at least a hundred years ahead of his time. Great interest is still shown by the number of people who come to visit the Factory and the School of Character where the families and workers received their education.

This is, I regret to say, the last book George Blake was to write as, unfortunately, he died when he had practically completed it and we shall not see any more of his interesting books and novels dealing with Glasgow and its environs.

I know that a tremendous amount of information about the Company has been obtained from our pensioners and older people in Port Glasgow who had sidelights on the Company and what it had done.

H E Semple

Chairman and Managing Director

Old Gourock from Battery Point. The original Ropework is clearly seen left centre.

Chapter I

FROM GOUROCK TO PORT GLASGOW

It is a summer evening on the Firth of Clyde. The sun is setting in a blaze of saffron, red and violet behind the splendid peaks of Argyll, and its light is still bright on the Renfrewshire moorlands, turning the green of the young heather to gold, the rocky outcrops to the likeness of shining ore. A mild sou'-westerly wind is blowing up past the outlying islands—Arran, Bute and the Cumbraes—from the open sea. It is an hour of peace, the serenity broken only by the creaking of spars and the whip of cordage, and by the shouts of men working about boats at the water's edge.

I

This is Gourock Bay, a nook of the Firth admirably sheltered from the prevailing wind by the ridge of Kempock Point about which the tidal Clyde turns southwards towards the Atlantic. The fishermen are clearing their craft from what seems like an artificial embankment but is, in fact, a huge pile of empty mussel shells, blue-black and pearl, built up by generations of inshore line fishermen needing the pink flesh for bait. The boats now moving out of Gourock Bay are sizeable sailing vessels, however. The long sweeps are pulling them by the score out into the fairway where their brown sails will take the wind round the point and carry them towards the shoals of herring that have been reported to be thick in the deep water. It is likely that many of the rough men at the oars have walked round Granny Kempock, the tall stone on the spur of the ridge, muttering pagan runes and praying that the local coven of witches has not laid an evil spell to break their hopes of fair weather and bulging nets....

So it may have been during the reign of Charles the Second, and now, 300 years later, there is no fishing for herring out of Gourock. The little town that grew about the cluster of fishermen's huts is largely residential, and the whole of one side of Gourock Bay is a railway terminal and a pier for the Clyde coast steamers. The bay is a yacht anchorage. That ancient activity in herring fishing, however, was the making of an industry, now huge in its ramifications. We should understand at the same time that the Clyde herring fisheries were huge in terms of the Scottish economy while the Merrie Monarch reigned.

A local historian, George Crawford, brought out his 'Description of Renfrewshire' in 1710 and wrote thus of the great days:—

'The Herring which are caught there being larger, firmer, and of a better taste and taking better with the salt than any other the Kingdom affords, are more valued, both fresh and salted, at home and abroad. When the fishing was considerable in the River Clyde there have been boats employed in catching Herrings about 900, built after the form of little galleys, each boat having on board four men and 24 nets, every net being six fathoms long, and a fathom-and-a-half in breadth, all joined together, making a considerable length. Anciently, none were allowed to fish to the 25 July about which time the shoals used to come from the sea which is called Lochin; and such as went a-fishing before that day were liable to a certain pecunial mulct. I understand that, anciently, the boats went a-fishing three times a year, which times were called the Drave; and there was payable to the Crown, out of each boat, of such a bigness as was then determined, a thousand Herring each Drave, and were afterwards paid by a measure of a fixed size and bigness from which that duty came to be called the Assyze Herring; which, by Act of Parliament in the reign of King James III, was annexed to the Crown.'

2

Crawford's antique phrase, 'taking better with the salt than any other the Kingdom affords', means, of course, that the Clyde herring was specially well suited for curing for export in barrels. His figure of 900 boats engaged in the Clyde fishing would seem to imply that they were all locally owned, but it is more likely that when the 'drave' caused this large number to assemble in the Firth, many came from the West Highlands and Islands, even from Northern Ireland and the Isle of Man: just as in present times it is a fleet of highly mixed origins that follows the herring in their mysterious seasonal movement from about the mouth of the Firth of Clyde and right round the North of Scotland until the last catches are brought into the East Anglian ports in late autumn.

However that may be, the Clyde-based 'herring busses' were sufficiently numerous to create a demand for nets, cordage and sailcloth. The rude fisherman of the 17th century may have had the skill to fashion his own net, but he could not manufacture the twine, and all the tools of his trade were vulnerable in storm and even less tempestuous conditions of the sea. It is the business of this history to show how one concern, founded in the 18th century in Gourock, to make ropes and canvas, has survived and vastly expanded to become a world power in that field of manufacture.

It is tolerably certain that every reader of this history, layman or expert, has at one time or another observed the legend, The Gourock Ropework Co. Ltd., Port Glasgow, even if only with a vague, subconscious interest. He, or she, may have seen it on the fabric of an army tent, on the walls of the 'Big Top' at a circus, on the proofed canvas cover over the load of a long-distance lorry, or even on the awning above a shop window. If the trade name could be woven into rope and cordage, the observer would see it in the hawsers of the *Queen Mary* as his or her great-great-grandparents could have seen it in the ropes supplied in 1812 for Henry Bell's pioneer steamboat, the *Comet*.

To many readers, again, the place-names concerned—Gourock and Port Glasgow—may seem remote. Even to those who know something of the district it must appear strange that The Gourock Ropework Company should have Port Glasgow, some six miles away, as the main base of its operations. This geographical, or topographical, oddity is in fact one key to an understanding of the Company's long and romantic evolution from a small local concern into one of international power.

3

Gourock and Port Glasgow are separate communities, each with its own local authority, at the western and eastern ends respectively of the long straggle of what is nowadays called a conurbation, the large burgh of Greenock in between. Greenock shelters some 80,000 inhabitants, Port Glasgow about 20,000 and Gourock only about 8,000. It might be thought by the outsider that these three burghs could usefully unite to form a whole with city status, but more than one attempt by Greenock to absorb its smaller neighbours provoked passionate opposition and fell down before the detachment of Parliament.

If, however, local patriotism runs strong in all three communities, they are willy-nilly bound in their fates by the fact that, in their cramped positions under the steep foothills of Renfrewshire, they face the anchorage known to mariners all over the world as The Tail of the Bank. This is the innermost point of deep-sea anchorage within the great natural harbour of the Firth of Clyde. It commands the approaches to Glasgow and the very heart of industrial Scotland from the West. Does even a very young reader need to be told that the Firth of Clyde was the very gullet of Britain during the worst years of the Second World War?

Despite the richness of the Clyde herring fisheries, these ports of West Scotland developed slowly and belatedly. Until towards the end of the 17th century none of them was little more than a huddle of fishermen's huts. Sir John Schaw of Greenock got from Charles I in 1635 the privilege of having the community rated as a burgh of barony, and he had a stone pier built for the benefit of the local fishermen and those who traded with Ireland. His son, also John, who had fought with the Cavaliers at Worcester, succeeded in having a proper harbour with the appropriate quays completed by 1710.

He did not do so without incurring a dangerous rivalry. Already in 1659, the Magistrates of Glasgow had carefully 'sighted the harberie of Newark': that is, the hamlet only a mile or two eastwards of Sir John Schaw's bailiwick. Less than 30 years later they acquired this land. Battle was joined. Glasgow was determined to have a port of its own, and it was going to have no truck with upstart Greenock. This intense trade war lasted for just over 100 years.

The position of the magistrates and merchants of Glasgow—and the terms were practically interchangeable—was difficult. Here was an ironical case of a country's busiest manufacturing centre almost baffled to find ways and means of getting its imports and exports from and to

4

a good harbour. The city, then a more beautiful place than it is now, was at the bridgehead of the River Clyde indeed, but between Glasgow Bridge and the nearest good anchorage opposite Greenock there stretched fully 20 miles of sandbanks—or 'hairsts'—and many obtrusive rocks in the bed of the steam. A limited amount of goods and a small number of passengers could be carried up and downstream in lighters or what were called flyboats, but that at the grave risk of being stranded on a sandbank for hours on end.

Over the course of many years the Glasgow magistrates struggled to loosen the topographical halter round their necks. At one point they were sending their continental trade through Bo'ness on the Firth of Forth, that route involving heavy overheads in the way of road transport. They made a pass at inducing the magistrates of Dumbarton to give them harbour facilities and were turned down on the ground that an influx of foreign seamen would disturb the peace of that ancient Royal Burgh and raise the price of provisions to the inhabitants. Another move to secure a foreport at Irvine on the Ayrshire coast also failed. The outcome of a long and complex story was the decision of Glasgow to create a port of its own, and that near Greenock.

The moves in the game that ensued were dramatic and picturesque, if occasionally amusing, as we see them nowadays. The eager men of Glasgow got themselves involved in all manner of squabbles with other authorities they thought to be denying them their rights *de facto* if not *de jure*. In one of their tussles with those stubborn Schaws of Greenock they lost by only a shade when the enemy pounced to buy from Lord Cochrane a piece of coastal territory they had coveted at Cartsburn, midway between Newark and the Schaw dominions. Thus thwarted, they returned to that 'harberie at Newark', and in 1688 they agreed with Sir Patrick Maxwell of Newark, with the consent of his wife, Dame Marion Campbell, and of his eldest son, Sir George Maxwell, to lease some 13 acres of flat land on the Newark estate. They got it at a bargain price—a capital sum of 1300 merks Scots and an annual feu duty of 4 merks: all the more a bargain since this flat bit of ground on the shores of the Clyde was fertile and supported some profitable market gardens. The sum of 1300 merks Scots was in 1688 the equivalent of only about £73—but money values have changed in over 200 years.

Newark Castle still stands within a stone's throw of the head office of The Gourock Ropework Company. It cannot be seen from the main

Glasgow–Greenock road, being nowadays lost behind the brick buildings and gantries of shipyards. The pedestrian must seek it out by a narrow lane; the hurrying motorist never thinks of it. It is nevertheless a lovely old Scots mansion-house, its stone dark red where it broods over the tidal waters of the Clyde, an Ancient Monument in the care of H.M. Ministry of Works.

Newark Castle was abandoned by its aristocratic owners in the early 18th century and declined in condition and importance. Indeed, it was mainly occupied by a series of market gardeners who had taken leases of Lord Belhaven's fine grounds, now all built over. One of these worthies used the banqueting hall as a store for apples and, to the puzzlement of later antiquarians, cut holes in the stone floor to take uprights that, boarded together, would contain his stores of fruit. By another character the kitchen premises were put to a stranger use. One day in 1830 there appeared in the *Glasgow Herald* an advertisement which ran:—

FOR SALE

A YOUNG LEOPARD, Six Months Old;

Likewise a Bear, Eight Months old.

Apply (if by letter, post paid)

to Mr. John Orr, rope maker,

Port Glasgow.

It was apparently this original's practice to go round the harbours and buy such animals as the sailors brought in from foreign parts. If it could be established, it would be interesting to know if he plied his more conventional trade in The Gourock's ropewalk.

The hamlet grouped about this castle had shared to some extent in the herring trade that had so greatly advantaged its neighbours downstream, but it had already been under the influence of Glasgow to some extent. It was the point at which much of the barge-borne merchandise for and out of Glasgow had been transferred from and into deep-water ships—too many of these ships Dutch for the liking of the Glasgow merchants. It had also some importance as a collecting centre for the salmon fisheries of the Clyde. These were important in those days, the big, silvery fish able to swim through clean water up to and through metropolitan Glasgow: so important that the values of the salmon fishings are specifically mentioned in all the older charters dealing with the transfer of riparian lands in the region.

Now, however, Glasgow was going to turn Newark into a busy fore-port, and it went about its task with vigour. The trade war was on. The Glasgow magistrates built at Newark a tidy harbour. They built a graving dock, the first in Scotland, the necessary power to empty it provided by horses pulling beams to turn the pump. Finally, they defeated Greenock by having their Custom-house at Port Glasgow (originally Newport Glasgow) rated as the principal Excise office on the Clyde.

This last success may represent Glasgow's superior power—or power of lobbying—in Parliament. The reader is merely asked to remember that Scotland had then still her own Parliament, the Estates, sitting in Edinburgh. The country's commercial situation had been only slightly alleviated by the Union of the Crowns in 1603; even Stuart monarchs could not browbeat the English merchants. When the Parliaments were united in 1707, however, the picture was changed completely, much to the economic advantage of Scotland as a whole, vastly to the advantage of those who traded out of the Clyde.

Suddenly the English Colonies had become the British Colonies; suddenly the trade routes were open to Scottish merchants and mariners. As the new possibilities were seen from the Clyde, the rosiest was the prospect of new trades across the Atlantic with the Americas. These possibilities were seized, and the Clyde ports started to expand—sugar, timber and tobacco being brought in huge quantities for processing. (The wars with France, allowing privately owned vessels to harry enemy shipping under Letters of Marque, were a highly profitable side-line over many years and founded the fortunes of many a now respected family). The new harbours were filled with shipping. The local boat-builders became shipbuilders, turning from modest herring busses to brigs capable of crossing the Western Ocean with goodly cargoes and their meed of passengers.

These were good times while they lasted. Gourock never developed as a port for shipping of size, and before the end of the 18th century its bay was declining in importance as a base for the fishing fleet, the herring shoals tending to move out into the deeper waters of the outer Firth of Clyde, into Loch Fyne and the Kilbrannan Sound. Port Glasgow and Greenock, however, and even in rivalry that fell just short of hostility, 'boomed' merrily. But this was for a relatively short space of historical time. If the new prosperity had come with the Union of the Parliaments in 1707, it was nearing its end with the outbreak of the

8

A View of Port Glasgow from the South East

American War of Independence in 1775, however much wealth the Napoleonic Wars were to bring into the Clyde for another short 'boom' period, as artificial and basically unsound as all flares of war-time prosperity are apt to be.

One sees now how vulnerable were the positions of Gourock, Greenock and Port Glasgow as against the wealth, power and ambitions of the Glasgow magistrates. These worthies had suffered a grievous blow when the victory of the American Colonists ruined their great tobacco trade with Virginia. The Tobacco Lords could no longer strut the Trongate in the red cloaks of their arrogance, but still they pressed on to realise the dream they had long cherished—that of so deepening the Clyde that ocean-going ships could by-pass the outports, even their own Port Glasgow, and bring the imports and carry away the exports from the doors of their own warehouses.

The story of Glasgow's unresting struggle to tame the Clyde, so to speak, has often been told: how huge sums of money were spent and the best civil engineering brains of the 18th century employed in discovering ways and means of fashioning a ship-channel from the open sea to the bridgehead. It is enough that they eventually succeeded. In 1806, the *Harmony* of Liverpool, 120 tons, moved up the new channel on the spring tide and tied up at the Broomielaw.

From that moment the days of Port Glasgow as a major West Coast harbour were numbered. As early as 1808 the Glasgow authorities sold their graving dock at the port to a local body. In due course they surrendered all their authority in the satellite town to a local council ... and it must have been a bitter thing for the Port Glasgow folk to see the big ships pass their harbour entrance on the way upstream.

But even though deprived of the direct patronage of the magistrates of Glasgow, the small town of Port Glasgow was not by any means killed by the removal of their patronage. For one thing, the association with the great city, however brief, had encouraged good men in the port to own and manage ships of their own, and Port Glasgow-owned ships profitably sailed the seas until towards the end of the 19th century. Much more important, the connection had fostered the growth of a lusty shipbuilding industry, and Port Glasgow's annual contribution to world tonnage is still a large one. Finally, the age of steam had still to come, and even if the local fishing fleets had dwindled by the turn of the century, the growing Clyde fleet of sailing ships required vast quantities

The old Harbour at Norfolk, Virginia.

of canvas, ropes, hatch covers and the like. Thus Port Glasgow boasted among its staple industries that of which The Gourock Ropework Company was the largest producer, now one of the largest producers in the world.

Why The Gourock Ropework Company should be operating in Port Glasgow is a small puzzle simply solved. In 1736 a group of Glasgow merchants, including a future Lord Provost of that city, Lawrence Dinwiddie, set up in Port Glasgow the Port Glasgow Rope and Duck Company. Some 40 years later another group of merchants, mostly from Greenock, established The Gourock Ropework Company on the shores of that little town's sheltered bay. Both enterprises prospered, but in 1797 the partners in the Port Glasgow Rope and Duck Company sold to their rivals the ropewalk and mills they had set up near Newark Castle; and so the Gourock men were left in a dominant position, with ropewalks and mills on two sites six miles apart, as it were straddling the long range of harbours and shipyards that had been created within 100 years or so.

Fortunately, some of the earliest Letter and Minute Books of both concerns have survived the assaults of time, and from the crabbed writing and antique phrases on the yellowing pages we can now appreciate the conditions in which, from 1736 to the present day, a huge organisation grew out of the merger of the Port Glasgow Rope and Duck Company with The Gourock Ropework Company more than 160 years ago.

The original Ropework building at Gourock. The tall building, centre, is still in existence as an Artisans' Club and overlooks Gourock Bay.

Chapter II

FOUNDATIONS OF TRADE

The first document bearing on the history of The Gourock Ropework Company is, in fact, the first Letter Book of the Port Glasgow Rope and Duck Company. The first entry is dated December 21st, 1736, the last August 23rd, 1746.

This volume, bound in leather and in a fair state of preservation, is of the size known to the stationery trade as Royal Quarto. The paper is of good legal quality, and the ink of nearly 250 years ago, though turned brown, has lasted wonderfully well. The letters were all signed by John Stevenson, the first manager of the Rope and Duck Company, but they seem to have been copied into the book by a series of clerks of highly varied standards of education. Some of the spellings are hilarious in our modern view, and some of the handwriting styles might well ruin the

13

eyesight of the research student. Even so, the sturdy business-like attitudes of John Stevenson are reflected clearly in this correspondence from the Port Glasgow office, and though he could not have known it, he left behind in these books a valuable record, not only of the early days of the company in particular, but also of the natures of Scottish trade during the turbulent 18th century.

Many of these letters, rendering John Stevenson's accounts of his stewardship, are addressed to Messrs Oswald, Dinwiddie, Brown & Company, merchants in Glasgow; and in the absence of any other documents, it is a fair inference from the tone of these communications that he was addressing his employers, the original partners in the Port Glasgow Rope and Duck Company. Lawrence Dinwiddie was to become a Lord Provost of Glasgow, and so also was Richard Oswald. Indeed, the latter's eminence in the affairs of the city is commemorated in the name of a busy street in the business heart of the modern city. There is no great intrinsic interest in the correspondence of the manager in Port Glasgow with head office in Glasgow proper, but it is perfectly clear from the general drift of Stevenson's letters, reporting progress and asking for instructions, that Oswald and Dinwiddie were the principals among his employers.

It is worth remembering that these letters, between places only 20 miles apart, took a long time on the way. They went by post, but the fastest journey by coach or on horseback must have occupied the best part of three hours. Thus a consultation between Stevenson and his employers may have occupied at least three days as against the few minutes on the telephone that would suffice in our modern times. It is even more important to remember that, in the choicest parts of his correspondence, John Stevenson was dealing with people hundreds and thousands of miles overseas, and that through the agency of small sailing vessels which took weeks and months on their voyages, with the possibility of total loss in storm all too near at any time.

The first three letters in the book are hard to decipher; the page has been torn across, and the ink has faded. The task of getting the sense of them with patience and a magnifying glass is, however, rewarding. It is seen at once that the correspondence deals almost entirely with trade overseas. The first letter of all, addressed to 'Mr George Cruickshank, at the house of Mr John Cruickshank, mercht in London', refers to his report on 'the State of trade at Pettersborgh'. The second, to 'Mr Peter

Barkaly, Mercht in Konnagsberg'—and these are literal transcriptions—is concerned with the supplies and prices of hemp at the Baltic ports, John Stevenson signing himself 'your oblidged and humbale Svt'. The third was addressed to a Mr Ralph Rodger in Rotterdam and has to do with the loss of a ship and therefore of goods exchanged between the correspondents.

It seems a reasonable inference that this Letter Book was kept mainly for correspondence with and about overseas concerns, and we may safely assume that trade with local shipowners and the regional herring fleet was conducted in personal contact. There were not a great many of these foreign letters in any one year, but we do well to remember that the Baltic, with which so much business was done, is frozen over for four months in each year.

The broad pattern of that commerce is clear. The Clyde exported salt herrings in large quantities, and the Port Glasgow company imported large quantities of hemp for its rope and sailcloth manufacturers. At the same time, John Stevenson's letters show that he was always anxious to pick up any odd bit of carrying trade that would fill up the empty spaces in the ships owned or chartered by the company. It is nowhere made clear how in fact these vessels were owned, but a survey of the correspondence suggests that there were usually four ships coming and going between the Clyde and the Baltic during the ice-free season. For the rest, there is only one hint in Stevenson's letters over more than ten years that his employers thought of having a ship built in Boston, Mass., and that reference stands alone and unexplained. On the other hand, quite the longest letter in the book is an acrimonious one, addressed to a firm in Saltcoats, Ayrshire, concerning a dispute over the charter of one of their vessels.

The bulk of the correspondence in the early years is with agents in the Baltic ports—David Barklay in Koenigsberg, Napier & Hasenfiller, then Prescott & Leake, in St Petersburg. It is mainly concerned with shipments outwards of those inevitable salted herring, with odd loads of salt in quantity. The incoming cargoes were almost invariably of hemp, flax and similar goods, with odd parcels of tar and barley. Small parcels of Russian woven fabrics were expressly ordered by Stevenson from time to time so that he might have a good look at the methods of his foreign friends and rivals. We learn with interest that a son of Barklay in Koenigsberg was employed at Port Glasgow, learning the rope and duck trade, and that his devotion to duty was commended at intervals. One oddity is that the word 'freight' is invariably spelt 'fraught' in these letters, and that when a vessel was loaded it was 'fraughted'. This may have been merely a regional pronunciation.

The Baltic traffic had an amusing domestic side. Mr. Barklay in Koenigsberg at one time wanted chairs and tables, and we may imagine these to have come out of the furniture factories of Beith or Lochwinnoch, set up to use the fine hardwoods then coming from Central America through Greenock. Again he requires a consignment of bonnets, the blue Kilmarnock bonnets then a speciality of that Ayrshire town. Most comically of all he asks that a 'Gray hound Dog and Bitch' be sent out, a commission Stevenson had some difficulty in executing.

From his own side the manager in Port Glasgow now and again solicited a luxury for himself and friends . . . 'If good prest Cavear can be had with you, please send me 10 lb. weight of it, which charge to account'. That was to Prescott and Leake in St Petersburg. On the same day he was writing to Barklay in Koenigsberg, 'Please send by Captain Duncan 10 pound of the best Cavear which charge to my account, and a bagg of Struggion, which charge also'. It is otherwise indicated that he requires some of the caviare for Mr Richard Oswald, merchant in Glasgow; and that seems to show beyond argument that Oswald was one of his employers and patrons. The request for Struggion—that is, sturgeon—indicates that the taste of the merchants of Clydeside was becoming eclectic. One looks, but in vain, for a reference to vodka.

It is still more interesting in terms of history that this Rope and Duck Company in Port Glasgow was corresponding with firms and agents far off the obvious Baltic route. One curious letter is addressed to a firm of merchants with the unusual name of William & Parr Thomsone in Cork, Ireland—or so the legend seems to read. This indicates that the men in Port Glasgow were to borrow from the Irish firm an operative who would come across and demonstrate the craft of weaving canvas—spelt 'canvass'. That was in 1741, and it seems probable that it was in this year that Port Glasgow first improved its methods of making canvas as well as cordage. The Irish firm were to find and supply the necessary machinery; their demonstrator was to be paid at the rate of £40 a year and found a decent house. John Stevenson signed himself 'Yr. much obliged and very humble Servt'.

There is a rather special interest in this passage. Ireland did have in those days a large rope and sailcloth industry, founded mainly by Huguenot refugees. Later on we shall see how this association with the people in Cork may have had a prophetic significance.

The letters finally demonstrate the importance of the North American connection after the Union of the Parliaments. So far as the Port Glasgow Rope and Duck Company was concerned, these links were firm by the 1740's. John Stevenson corresponded with merchants and agents in Philadelphia, Boston, Annapolis and Norfolk, Virginia. One quite short letter to 'Captain James Bayly of Scooner *Nelly* of Glasgow' instructs him explicitly to proceed without loss of time to Boston 'in new England', there discharge his cargo 'agreeable to Bills of Lading', and then proceed to 'Rapahanock in Virginia', there to pick up a cargo of 'Tobacco directly for Clyd'; and Mr. Stevenson wishes his correspondent all the best for a 'healthy and a happy Return'. This and other entries usefully demonstrate the importance of the Glasgow tobacco trade and suggest that Oswald and Dinwiddie were among the Tobacco Lords as well as partners in a rope and sailmaking concern.

The Letter Book kept by John Stevenson indirectly records the decline of the herring fisheries in the upper Firth of Clyde. In December 1736, he wrote Barklay at Koenigsberg rather tamely to the effect that ... 'when we send our vessell in the spring have some thought of sending a quantity of herrings by her, and you may depend on them being well taken caire of, as we shall repack them all ourselves'. Three months later he is writing in a minor key ... 'there is no herring fished in Clyde. Lochfyne is the nearest place to us where any quantity are made, and we think these Herrings caught at the Isles (which is opposite to the Lewes) full as good as Lochfines and not any difference in the price'.

He is more cheerful in April 1737, advising Barklay ... 'I have sent you thirty and three Last and 7 Barells of fine Herrings and hope from your former advises will come to a very good market'. Towards the end of 1738 he seems to have given up the export of herring as a bad job, reporting ... 'Our herring fishing has been very badd, which has been a great loss to these parts'; and soon we hear that he is sending lead, apparently mined in the Highlands, to his friend in Koenigsberg.

Those morose passages invite some comment and explanation. A last of herrings contained twelve barrels. Loch Fyne is a branch of the Firth of Clyde. Stevenson was surely disingenuous in suggesting that

the herring caught about the Outer Isles were as good as the genuine Loch Fynes; these have kept their singularly high quality and reputation into the 20th century. It is clear, however, that the herrings which provided Gourock with its staple trade in the 17th century were moving into the outer waters before the middle of the 18th. It is also a reasonable conclusion that the Port Glasgow Rope and Duck Company had by then come to depend on the sale of its goods to ocean-going vessels rather than to small herring busses in home waters.

And then, during anxious months in 1745–46, Lawrence Dinwiddie and Richard Oswald as merchants in Glasgow were dragged into the main stream of British history and, as partners in the Port Glasgow Rope and Duck Company, forced to pay tribute to the leaders of an army of rebellion.

At the head of the Highland Host the Young Pretender, Bonnie Prince Charlie, halted twice in Glasgow, both on his way south in September 1745, and on the return from Derby—and towards defeat at Culloden in January 1746. On both occasions he demanded large sums of money and large supplies of goods from the unsympathetic

18

citizens. Oswald and Dinwiddie, as leaders within the community, were no doubt mulcted in cash as well as goods, and possibly the canvas required from the Port Glasgow Rope and Duck Company was a moiety of their ransom. At all events, the Company was obliged to supply nine and one-half pieces of cloth for the protection of the Pretender's baggage train. A piece of cloth is a bolt of from 60 to 100 yards in length. This demonstrates at least that the Q department of the Jacobite army knew its business very well, and that the Highlanders were more than the 'rabble' of the Hanoverian historians.

It had already fallen to John Stevenson in Port Glasgow to write, without knowing it, the very stuff of British history. This was in a letter addressed to Andrew Sprewll, merchant in Norfolk, Virginia, dated October 10th, 1745, and reproduced below:—

To Mr. Andrew Sprewll,
    Merchant in Norfolk, Virginia.   P. May.

Dear Sir:
    Referring to what I wrote you by the 'Leah', & 'Elizabeth Hastie', since arrived, the 'Elizabeth Giles', 'Boyd', 'Mattie & Pegge', with your 'Triton' & two Liverpoole ships, you will please, if you have not already done it, send us an exact state of the money paid into Mr Harvie and Mr Duncan Graham and at what Exchange they have accounted for said money, for we look on ourselves, I mean the Ropework Compy., to have nothing to do with the present Exchange, in such parcels of Riggen sent on commission but expect our money remitted us Sterling, agreeable to the invoice sent. We shall expect to hear from you by the 'Jenny', not yet arrived, and hope you have advised if we shall send you another assortment of Riggen or Sailcloth. I hope on the Leah's arrival she will meet with dispatch, having wrote you to load her with 120 barrels Pitch, 120 barrels Turpentine & 560 barrels Tar of the best Browny kind providing Mr B. O. Jun. now at London does not order the contrarie before she arrives. I can send you no newspapers, all these being laid aside, at least do not come to our hands as usuall. Our country in ye utmost confusion, all trade at a standstill, and people in terror— about 25th July the Pretender's eldest son, Pr. Charles landed with 5 men only in ye Highlands. Has since gathered to a numerous army. On 17th Sept. they gott possession of Edinburgh. On the 21st of said mo. they routed Sir John Cope, neare Prestonpans, having killed in ye action 500, taken 1,400 prisoners & 900 wounded, possess'd of all their baggage and artillery, it's said the Highdrs. were about 4,000, the 1,500 not engagd. This is a very compleat victory. Since they have been aiming at the Castle where there is a great treasure, but to no effect. They now lie encampd near Diddington & are said to be 8,000, some say 10,000 strong, well fitted in every things & said accounts from London say vigorous methods are taking to destroy them, that Genls. Wade and Cholmondly are already near Berwick, the first with 12,000 fine troops, the other with 4,000, and a grand

To Mr Andrew Sprewll Merchant in, Norfolk as a .... by May

Sir Referring to what I wrote you by the Leah, & Eliz at Maderas, since arrived the Elisabeth Isles, Boyd Mader Spegg with ye Fiston & 2 Liverpool Ships you will please if you have not already done it, Send us an Exact State of the money paid into Mr Parvie & Wm Pare on fore home and at what Exchange they have recovered for said money, for we look on our selves, I mean the Roperk Compy to have nothing to do with the present Exchange, in Such parcels of Riggen Sent on Commission But Expect our money remitted us Stealing agreeable to the Invoice Sent We Shall Expect to hear from you by the Jenny, not yet arrived and hope you have advice of we Shall Send you another assortment of Riggon or Sailcloth I hope on the Leahs arrivall She will meet with all Dispatch having wrote you to load her with 120 Bleh, wd Sup ontwo & 50 .... of the Best Bowry head, providing Mr W. Fitr ... at London does not order the Contrarie before She arrives. I can Send you no news papers all these being .... order, as least do not come to our hand, as usual. our Country in .... utmost Confusion, all Trade at a Stand and people in Terror. about 25 July the Pretenders Eldest Son for Earle landed with 5 men only in ye Highlands, he Since gathered to a Numerous Army, On 17 Sept. they got possession of Edr. on the 21 of said ma they routed St. Johns Cope. Ihre are p..stonians having kill ..... killed 500 taken 1400 prisoners & 900 wounded possessed of all their Baggage & artillery. ... and the high men were about 8000 the 1500 not Engag'd, this was a Compleat victory. Since they have been ...... at the castle ... and there's a great Treasure but we Effect they now ly Encampd near Dittington & are Said to be 8000 Some Say 10000 Strong, will fall in Every thing but Accounts of our extraordinary Rigorous methods we taking to Destroy them. that Genll Wade & Cholmondly are advancing near Barwick ye first with 12000 Fine Troops, the other with 4000 and a Grand Train of Artillery, its pretty Easy to Guess the Consequences, in any Event .... this Country must Suffer greatly I only Strive to ..... things .... to be and to part .... would Every Friend to your —— I hereby wish you wth Esteem Respectfully Dear Sir

your very Humble Servt John Stevenson

In Glasgow Octr 10 1745

train of artillery. It's pretty easy to guess the consequences. In any event this country must suffer greatly. I only choose to give things in generall, to descend to particulars would be very tedious to you. I heartily wish you well & am,

Respectfully, dear sir,
Your very humble servt.
JOHN STEVENSON.
Manager.

Port-Glasgow, October 10th, 1745.

Mr Stevenson must have been in such a state of concern that his normal lucidity forsook him, or his clerk must have been shamefully careless in his copying. Even so, this is again the stuff of history, a report from a country in a state of civil war, and it is remarkable that it should have gone to the Americas from the pen of a ropework manager in a very small Scottish town.

The beginnings of The Gourock Ropework Company are outlined with more certainty than those of the Port Glasgow Rope and Duck Company it was to absorb in due course. Whereas John Stevenson's letter book is a fascinating document, presenting a wonderful picture of day-to-day business in the 18th century, the first document concerning The Gourock is its original Minute Book—or Sederunt Book, as it is labelled in the grave Scottish fashion. This contains a copy, running to 18 folio pages, of the Contract of Copartnery by which it was set up. The agreement was completed in June 1777.

The partners were Joseph Tucker; James Taylor; two John Campbells, senior and junior; two more Campbells, Colin and Neil; Robert Lee; John Cathcart; John Esdale; William Fullarton; John Buchanan, junior; Andrew Anderson; John Kippen; William Morrison and Alexander Laird. These are all formally described as Merchants in Greenock. There then follows the name of John Robertson, Merchant in Rothesay—that is, in the Isle of Bute. Finally, the consortium was completed by Alexander McCaul, Dugald Thomson and William Coats, Merchants in Glasgow.

That is: the first Gourock Ropework Company was formed by fifteen men of business from Greenock, one from Rothesay and three from Glasgow. The capital of the new company was £6,000. All save Alexander Laird were to be interested to the extent of one-twentieth of the total. Laird was to be the manager with a holding of one-fortieth along with a modest wage and some bonuses. Among nearly a score of men the investment cannot be thought heavy, even allowing for the vastly changed values of the pound as between 1777 and today.

Those who know something of the social and commercial history of Clydeside must find this list of the original proprietors profoundly engaging. Campbells were always thick on the ground in that region, to be sure. The names of Fullarton and Buchanan in particular were to be long prominent in the commercial life of Greenock, and we may see how the former surname persisted long in the domestic history of The Gourock Ropework Company. It is reasonable to assume that the William Coats of Glasgow was a progenitor of the family so closely associated with the Paisley thread industry. For some mysterious reason the Contract of Copartnery is signed by names that are not mentioned in the preliminary clauses of the document—Archibald Baine and John Armour & Co., for instance—and the Baines were long prominent in the affairs of Greenock as partners in a shipping firm that specialised in the trade with Newfoundland. Presumably some of those signing as individuals were also signing for the firms they represented.

It may seem a trifle irrelevant, but the signatures of all but one of the interested parties are remarkably graceful, suggesting that, if an 18th century man was educated, he was apt to be well-educated. The exception is that of Neil Campbell, his signature such a monstrously comic effort that one fancies he must have been very old or convivial in his habits and given to plying a much worn quill. He invariably spelt his christian name as 'Neill'.

The copartnery was set up 'to carry on a Joint Trade and Manufactory of Cordage and Sailcloth', having 'already contracted with Tradesmen for making a Ropewalk and building Houses and other necessary Conveniencies for carrying on the said Manufactory'. Their representatives had already agreed with Sir John Stuart of Castlemilk to feu a piece of land 'at the East End of the Town of Gourock'. Why a consortium of Greenock merchants with a few from Glasgow should choose to build a considerable place in Gourock is perhaps no great mystery. It is likely that they got the land cheap, as the magistrates of Glasgow had got the lands of Newark—and the non-Scottish reader may need to be reminded that the Scottish 'feu' is a wholly native form of contract whereby, with appropriate restrictions, the landlord lets out a plot of ground in perpetuity, and that usually without the passing of any capital sum.

22

Photostat of plan of Gourock dated 1721. Although no buildings are shown, it is interesting to that the site on which was built the original Gourock Ropework Company's ropewalk in 177 already marked 'Ropework' in 1721. At that time it was not uncommon to make rope in the of good weather and it may be that the real origins of The Gourock go back much further than the presently accepted as their date of establishment.
It may be noted that the accompanying map of early Gourock shows clear signs of town plat unfortunately never realised.

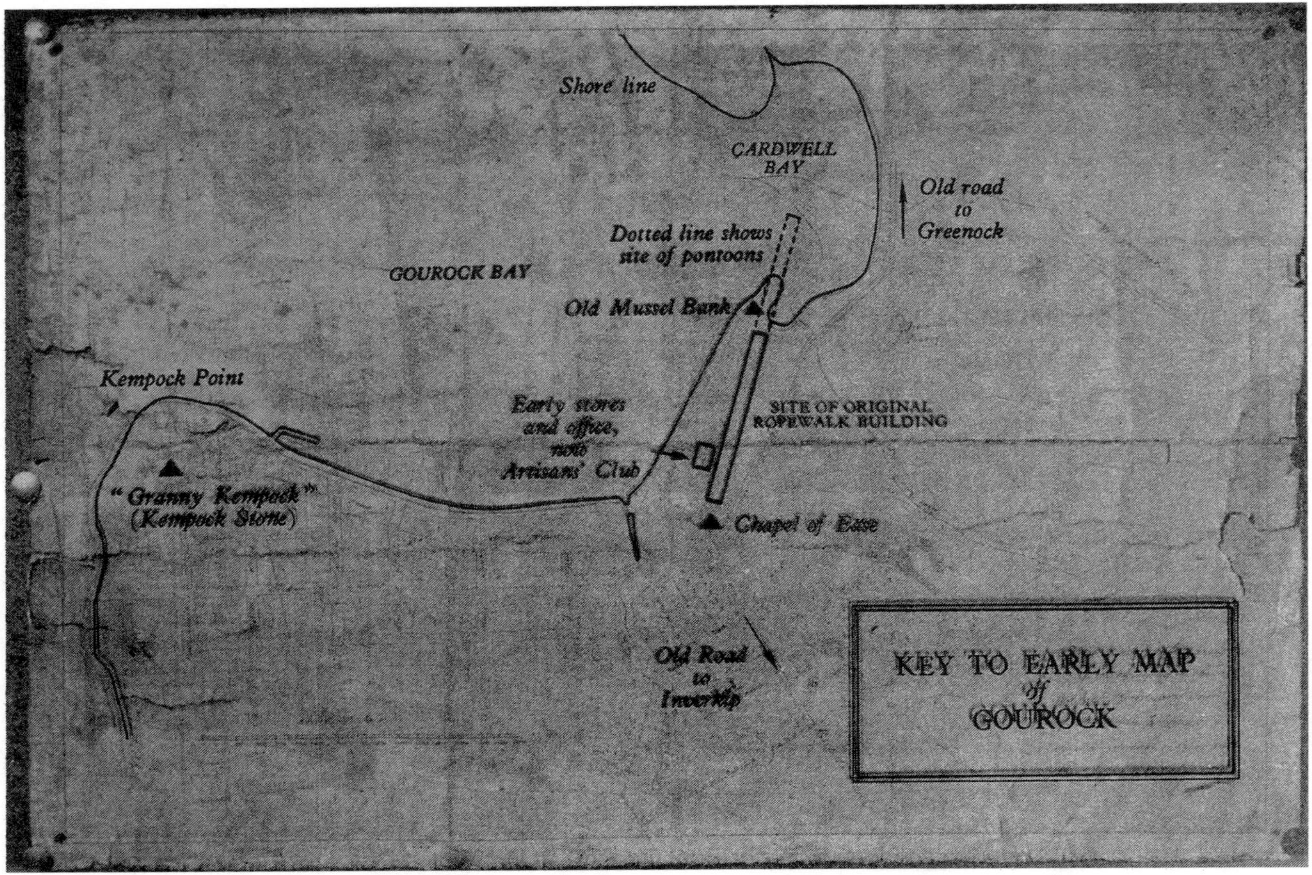

KEY TO EARLY MAP
of
GOUROCK

Shore line

CARDWELL BAY

Old road
to
Greenock

Dotted line shows
site of pontoons

GOUROCK BAY

Old Mussel Bank

SITE OF ORIGINAL
ROPEWALK BUILDING

Chapel of Ease

Early stores
and office,
now
Artisans' Club

Old Road
to
Inverkip

Kempock Point

"Granny Kempock"
(Kempock Stone)

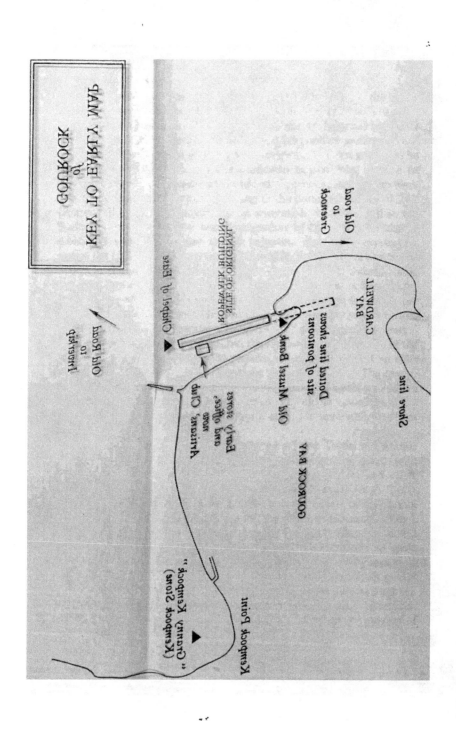

KEY TO EARLY MAP
of
GOUROCK

Old Road
to
Inverkip

Chapel of Ease

SITE OF ARKAVARK
BURIAL GROUND

Old road
to
Greenock

Shore line

CARDWELL
BAY

Dotted line shows
site of pontoons

Old Mussel Bank

Early store,
Coal office,
Artisans' Club

GOUROCK BAY

Kempock Point

"Kempock"
Granny Kempock
(Kempock Stone)

It is most likely that the site at Gourock was chosen for the simple reason that stretches of level land are scarce in that part of the world. It is almost certain that the choice was not made in relation to the herring fishing out of Gourock, for as we have already gathered from John Stevenson's correspondence, that industry had already moved away down the Firth of Clyde. It is merely possible that the original directors of The Gourock saw in the nearness of tidal water a cheap and convenient means of moving their raw materials inwards and their manufactured products outwards. This surmise seems to be supported by the fact that a Dry Dock is latterly listed among the company's assets, if valued at only £150.

Thus they set up their ropewalk on the shores of Gourock Bay. This inlet is really kidney-shaped, the larger, western lobe being Gourock Bay proper; the shallower, eastern branch is called Cardwell Bay. In fact, the original Gourock ropewalk, 200 fathoms long and slated for half its length, ran down to a rocky spit that marked the division between the two indentations.

The distinction has largely disappeared, for an esplanade nowadays runs in a series of curves above the foreshore, and the open land shown in the earlier picture of the Company's original works is covered with tenement buildings and some villas along the sea front. This building activity led in turn to the formation of streets running down to the sea, and finally the extension of the then Caledonian Railway to Gourock and the creation of a steamboat terminal at Kempock Point in 1889 altered the scene suggested by that charming old print.

It is still possible, however, to trace the general lines of the old establishment. It ran from the main Greenock–Gourock highway, near where the now busy road turns down a sharp hill into Gourock proper. A few of the old buildings have survived—the three-storey main building and a few extensions near the shore: the three-storey building housing an artisans' club, for instance, other flats of which were used from time to time as lofts for sails and other yachting gear, at one time by an earlier Ratsey, progenitor of the Ratsey side of the now famous firm of sailmakers, Ratsey and Lapthorne. The esplanade that curves round the twin bays is now Cove Road, but it was once Ropework Street.

The Gourock's original ropemakers could, and did in fact, easily extend their area of operation by hauling extra long strands beyond the foreshore and over pontoons moored in Cardwell Bay. On shore, heavier

A later view of Gourock from the south-east. Again the ropework building shows up prominently at left centre of the picture.

strands were hauled by donkeys and heavy ropes laid-up by donkey power.

The first Sederunt Book of The Gourock Ropework Company is not a notably exciting volume, very much less so than the Letter Book kept by John Stevenson in Port Glasgow. One gets the general impression of a reasonably prosperous business, prudently managed. All the many partners apparently did no more than attend the annual general meeting, the supervisory work being done by a committee of management of four or five of the partners, with a manager on the spot.

The Company was unfortunate in its first two managers. The first of all, Alexander Laird, appears to have got their affairs, or their books at least, into such a mess within less than two years that he had to be summarily dismissed and the annual balance postponed for a year. His successor, William Humphry, did not last the course for long thereafter. The appointment finally went to Archibald Baine, already a nominal partner—at a salary of £60 a year—and Baine's name is appended to all the minutes until the book closes.

Death changed the rota of partners from time to time, and now and again one or two of the weaker brethren hypothecated their shares against loans or bills—a practice so much disfavoured by their colleagues that they were obliged to resign. On the whole, however, neither the number of partners nor the individual holdings in the business varied greatly from year to year. The last balance sheet set out in the book—really a rather simple Profit and Loss account—reveals that in 1795 the company formed with a capital of £6,000 could reckon its total assets at nearly £28,000—considerable progress in less than 20 years. The accountant of today may be interested to know that this balance provided a reserve fund not only for bad debts but also another for 'doubtful debts'. The dividend on a sixteen and one-half share of £500 was £25, and this modest five per cent had been maintained over a period of years. The value of the £500 share was reckoned to be £763 6s. 8d.

The last entry in the book minutes the proceedings at a meeting held in the Bishopton Inn on October 7th, 1795; and if there is a temptation to think that this must have been a convivial occasion, let it be remembered that Bishopton was a convenient half-way house between Gourock and Glasgow. No doubt the decanters circulated, and one would like to have heard the broad Scots speech of these worthies in their knee breeches, worsted hose and flat-heeled shoes. This meeting had the serious purpose of discussing a dissolution of the original partnership. The proceedings seem to have been amicable, but nine of the original shareholders chose to withdraw; four from Greenock and all the representatives from Glasgow, including William Coats; and they were to be paid out in full. Eight men remained in the business, seven from Greenock and John Robertson of Rothesay. This minute reminds us that the consortium traded officially under the name of Campbells, Lee & Company, though all the earlier minutes refer to the affairs of The Gourock Ropework Company.

However amicable, the dissolution of partnership provokes one or two speculations. Was the ultimate acquisition of the Port Glasgow Rope and Duck Company in 1797 already envisaged in 1795? Did the Glasgow partners foresee that a feasible ship-channel would soon be open up the Clyde, and that they could safely draw out of their commitments twenty-odd miles downstream? But the minute book throws no light on these issues.

Two small but interesting points of mainly local interest remain. Among the assets at the balance of 1795 there is listed Aillay Mill valued at £179. Those who know the region intimately can only conjecture that this was the property now shown on the Ordnance Survey Map as Islay Mill, two or three miles over the hill from Gourock in the Kip Valley on the old road to the coast: a small farm until some 40 years ago and then rebuilt as a dwelling house for his retirement by a professional man from Greenock. It seems quite likely that The Gourock Ropework Company had a small subsidiary here, using the copious water power of the region and making worsted fabrics out of the wool of the large flocks of Blackface sheep on the hills above.

Where the main road from Greenock turns sharply downhill into Gourock proper, the wayfarer sees in the inner angle of the bend, and through a rather shabby thicket of funereal trees and untended shrubs, a number of tilted tombstones and the shards of a derelict building. This was the site, first, of a mere preaching station and then of a chapel-of-ease set up in 1776, hard by the original and primitive town-house of the Stuarts of Castlemilk and not far from the Gourock House subsequently built by the Darroch family that bought the estate in 1794. It is a fair enough inference that the chapel was placed there to serve the spiritual needs of the fishing village along the shore road and the population growing about the ropeworks. A local historian describes it thus:—

'It was a very small place of worship, with earthen floor, and only partially seated with rough benches. It had no vestry; and old Baldie Cameron, the rope-spinner, who rang the bell, had to perform his work standing in the corner of the little church amongst the congregation'.

Thus the description of the remote bellringer of a remote chapel, Archibald Cameron by name, pleasantly reinforces the identification of The Gourock Ropework Company with that small corner of the world. It is of some interest that the Company subscribed towards the cost of building a new Parish Church of Gourock in 1832. Although headquarters were transferred to Port Glasgow with the merger of 1797, the works at Gourock were not abandoned until 1851.

Henry I—Henry Birkmyre of Kilbarchan.

Chapter III

THE BIRKMYRES

On the last blank page of the Letter Book which John Stevenson kept so long on behalf of the Port Glasgow Rope and Duck Company there stands the legend, in somewhat untidy handwriting, 'Henry Birkmyre, 1792'.

There is nothing about it to explain why the name and date should have been noted in this curt and baffling fashion. It is as if, long after Stevenson's death and the closing of his book, somebody had been 'doodling', in the modern phrase. Examination of the later books of The Gourock Ropework Company suggests, however, that this was quite probably a note written by Henry Birkmyre himself when reading the Company's early correspondence in his own old age. In the absence of any written context the point cannot be proved, but a careful study of this man's signature on business documents strongly suggests that, his historical imagination stimulated by reading the old records of the firm, Henry Birkmyre thus recorded the beginning of his own connection with it.

As we shall see, he was to become a partner in The Gourock Ropework Company. It will also be shown that the chief ownership and control of this large concern came under the hands of his descendants and are so to this day. The Birkmyres are thus among the few families that, in Scotland, have remained in continuous family management of large businesses during the course of centuries. It is allowed that the Bank of Scotland, founded in 1695, is the country's oldest commercial concern, but a Bank is not a family business. The oldest in this family class are probably John Haig & Co. Ltd., of Markinch who, although not registered as a company until 1894, first started commercial distillation of whisky in 1627. They are followed somewhat later by Scotts' Shipbuilding and Engineering Company of Greenock, dating from 1711. Austin & McAslan, Ltd., agricultural seedsmen of Glasgow, follow quickly in 1717. The Gourock Ropework Company, tracing its origins back to the Port Glasgow foundation in 1736, comes fourth on this list and the Birkmyre connection has already lasted nearly 170 years.

How these Birkmyres originated, proliferated and prospered we shall shortly see; and it may be taken that the vast expansion of The Gourock Ropework Company during the 19th century and into the second half of the 20th was entirely the doing of this large, gifted and inveterately industrious family. It is necessary, however, to understand how, first, The Gourock Ropework Company managed its acquisition of the Port Glasgow Rope and Duck Company, and then, how the control of the business passed into those able Birkmyre hands.

The first Minute Book of the original Gourock Company stops short with an account of the meeting at Bishopton Inn and the reorganisation of the partnership. A new book was therefore ordered, and it also has fortunately survived fire, pulping and that sort of neglect which has overtaken too many historical records. This second is a very much ampler book than the first, and the handwriting throughout is infinitely more lucid than in the older record.

The first significant entry is dated September 15th, 1797, just after the Gourock-Port Glasgow merger, and it runs over the years until it ends with the minute of the annual meeting of 'seventeenth of May 1873'. (The Company's formal meetings were usually held in Greenock, the large town between the small towns of Gourock and Port Glasgow.) This book therefore presents a picture in clear outline of a remarkable expansion over a period of more than 70 years.

The first effective entry in this second Minute Book reveals that the Gourock company paid £1,720 for the assets of the Port Glasgow group. For a few years after 1797 the properties in Gourock were valued rather more highly than those at the Port. It is revealed also that the new partnership had acquired premises in Greenock, and since 'Goods on hand p. Inventory at Greenock' are listed as the largest asset apart from debts due to the Company, we may assume that this was a warehouse or transit depot; the largest of the three towns possessing the largest harbour and the largest fleet of shipping. Greenock was to become, and still is, a place of manufacture of the Company's products, but in 1797 that was still in the future.

The advance in the fortunes of The Gourock Ropework Company during the few years after the merger was of almost startling rapidity. The total wealth of the firm in 1797 was reckoned to be, in round figures, just short of £29,000. A year later they were reckoned to be nearly £39,000. By 1804 they had risen in value to just over £71,000. It seems reasonable to conclude that these phenomenal advances were due to heavy demands for naval equipment during the Napoleonic Wars. The value of any one share rose during the same brief period from £943 16s. to £3,874—allowing, of course, for a reduction in the number of partners by death or bankruptcy. But this second Minute Book does not declare, as did the first, how the profits of those golden years were divided among the partners.

Year by year the interests of the company were extended. In 1800 a cotton and barley mill in Port Glasgow—a curious conjunction of interests—was acquired, its value entered in the books at £850. Five years later a major expansion was put in hand, the decision minuted thus:—

'Mr Baine stated to the meeting the many disadvantages the Company labour under on account of being obliged to purchase all the yarn they have occasion for, for the Sailcloth Manufacture, and that when this branch of their business has so much increased, that it would be greatly to the interest of the Company to spin the yarns necessary for their Manufacture by which means, beside the profit that may reasonably be expected from this new Branch of Trade, the quality of their Sailcloth would be very much improved—that the Company's Ground and other conveniencies at Port Glasgow are well adapted for the purpose, and that the expense of erecting the Spinning Mill to be wrought by a Steam Engine on the Company's premises will be about Five thousand pounds'.

This somewhat breathless recommendation was approved at once, and Archibald Baine was empowered to enter into the appropriate negotiations. The boldness of the decision to use steam power in 1805 should be appreciated; even Watt's best engine was a clumsy, cranky thing at that stage. And it will be agreed that £5,000 was a heavy investment more than 150 years ago.

The flax spinning mill duly built, the installations at Port Glasgow began to take on in the annual accounts larger values than those in Gourock and Greenock. The Port Glasgow Ropework now appears as a separate entry beside a Sailcloth Manufactory with houses and lands attached. The mysterious Ailley Mill, having been written down to about £40, disappears from the accounts in 1806. By 1810 the business is valued at over £105,000, and in this year the declaration of a dividend is at last minuted—£630 on each share, the share worth £8,946 10s.

This increase in the value of the share was as before, partly due, however, to a gradual reduction in the number of partners. Some were removed by death in the nature of things, some by the sin of bankruptcy—Neill Campbell of the fantastic signature among the latter. On the whole, the tendency of the surviving partners was to close their ranks and increase their holdings in a concern so rapidly and greatly prospering. The heirs and agents of deceased partners were eager to get in on the ground floor, as the phrase goes. . . .

A novelist would find the material of a period tale in these curt records of industrial advance: perhaps noting such a touching little thing as the slow decline in the firmness of Archibald Baine's signature, until it becomes that of an old and failing man before it disappears from the minutes of 1843. He had given the Company sterling service since he became its manager in the early 1780's. He must be remembered as one of the founding fathers of The Gourock Ropework Company.

The Company had had to survive many crises before then, however. On one occasion the partners were obliged to borrow from the funds of the Parish Church to meet the wages bill. The ups and downs of its affairs during the first 30 years of the 19th century were almost fantastic in their vagaries. For example, the accounts for 1811 declared the assets to be nearly £110,000, and each share in that year was valued at £9,290, while the dividend was £1,290 per share. In 1826 the assets were reckoned to be worth only £43,000 and the dividend was down to £350: and then down to a meagre £120 in 1829. During the early 1830's the partners were sombrely considering the closing down of their works: at the best, an attempt to sell them.

The causes of these fluctuations seem obvious enough. The vast profit of 1811 was surely due to the 'boom' in overseas trade, made possible by the obliteration of the French fleet at Trafalgar in 1805. The setbacks of the 1820's were surely due to a condition of post-war 'slump'—often enough referred to in the Minute Book, though not in that term. A close reading of those minutes from year to year, however, suggests that too many of the partners were getting too old. It is quite obvious, though Archibald Baine's minutes are admirably crisp, that there was a good deal of jockeying for position among the diminishing

William I.

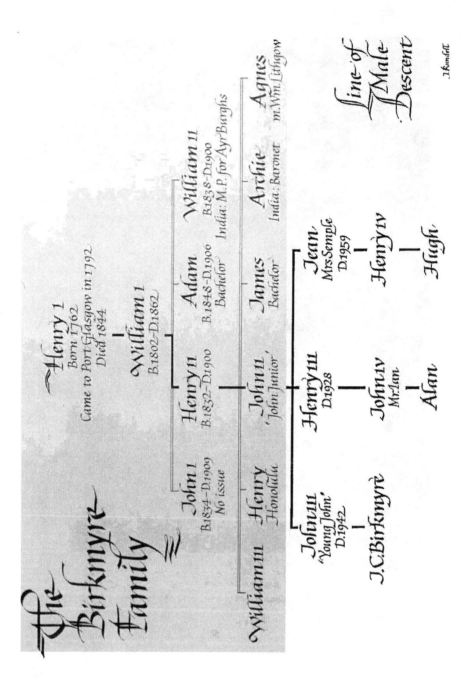

The Birkmyre Family

Henry I
Born 1762
Came to Port Glasgow in 1792
Died 1844

William I
B.1802–D.1862

John I
B.1834–D.1909
No issue

Henry II
B.1832–D.1900

Adam
B.1848–D.1906
Bachelor

William II
B.1838–D.1900
India: M.P. for Ayr Burghs

Archie
India: Baronet

Agnes
m. Wm. Lithgow

William III

Henry
Honolulu

John II
'John Junior'

James
Bachelor

Henry III
D.1928

Jean
Mrs. Semple
D.1959

John III
'Young John'
D.1942

John IV
Mr. Ian

Henry IV

J.C. Birkmyre

Alan

Hugh

Line of Male Descent

J. Russell

number of partners. By 1831 there were only four of them to sign the book; and in this situation lay the seeds of future conflict.

When Henry Birkmyre was assumed a partner in The Gourock Ropework Company in 1814 it was along with a colleague, David Johnstone. The appropriate minute describes the latter as 'manager at Port Glasgow' and the former as 'foreman there'. It is possible that these terms did not in 1814 connote the difference of status they would imply today, and Henry Birkmyre must have been a remarkable foreman to be so honoured. The transaction, however, allowed Johnstone to take up one half of a share, Birkmyre only one quarter: the share having been valued in that year at £6,628. Probably his quarter was all that a foreman, who had started as a simple weaver, could afford. Henry Birkmyre was able to raise his holding to one half of a share in 1824, but Johnstone and his heirs were able to keep ahead of the Birkmyres in financial power, and the ultimate disposal of the Johnstone interest was to be a somewhat troublesome matter.

In the meantime, Henry Birkmyre had had five children by his wife, Agnes. There were three sons, Henry, John and William; two daughters, Agnes and Jean. These male Christian names have survived in the family unto the seventh generation. The figure of the second son John does not appear on this documentary screen. The eldest, Henry, had his modest place in the affairs of The Gourock: he died unmarried. But the youngest of all, William, was a quite remarkable person, still recognised as the genius of the firm, the man under whose management the firm's production rose by leaps and bounds, and that while his father was still alive, he was appointed manager of the Sailcloth Department in 1827, when its output was 177,513 yards; the figure was over 900,000 yards when he went to take care of the Ropewalk. (It had risen to 1,751,000 yards by 1847.) The volume of rope sales under his hand grew from 6,972 cwts. in 1836 to 23,121 cwts. in 1847.

The nature of hereditary ability is a fascinating subject of study. He was obviously an unusual man this first Henry Birkmyre who, a simple weaver in the small Renfrewshire town of Kilbarchan, became foreman in a sizeable mill in Port Glasgow; only outstanding skill and character could have justified his election as a partner in 1814. Next comes a son of quite outstanding ability, William Birkmyre I, largely responsible for the expansion of the business and still able to play a part in public affairs as Provost of Port Glasgow. It will be shown that William's sons enlarged the positions he had created and in due course made the Birkmyres the predominant partners in the Company.

Birkmyre is an uncommon surname. Only six of the clan are listed in the Glasgow Telephone Directory, and one of these is in fact a member of the firm. There is in Dumfriesshire a small estate with the name of Birkmyre, but this may be a purely descriptive appellation, since 'birk' is good Scots for the common birch and 'myre' could be a bog or moss. Patiently traced, and usually spelt 'Birkmyr', the name turns up in some odd connections—a Michael Birkmyr, who was a presbyter of the Diocese of Glasgow in 1432; an Alexander Birkmyr, who witnessed a legal document in Glasgow in 1485; and Andrew Birkmyr, who was *Decanus* of Angus in 1517; and then—very interesting this—a George Birkmyre, in the modern spelling, who appeared in the course of a legal process at 'the Kirk of Inchynnane' in 1588.

This last reference is specially interesting because there has passed down the line of the Port Glasgow family of Birkmyres a legend to the effect that the founder of their line was a Huguenot, Johannes Berkemeyer, who came to Inchinnan in Renfrewshire in the company of a Scottish soldier of fortune called Rab Tamson, later marrying the latter's sister, Maggie, and eventually settling down as a weaver in Kilbarchan, only a few miles distant from Inchinnan. The grain of probability in this story is supplied by the appearance of a George Birkmyre at the Kirk of Inchynnane in 1588—that is, after the arrival of the Huguenot refugees in this country. But if we accept that reading of history, we have to admit that the Birkmyrs of the earlier Scottish records were certainly not Huguenots, even if an incoming Berkemeyer could conveniently change his surname to the native Birkmyre.

At the same time, the research branch of the Huguenot Society of London declares that Berkemeyer was almost certainly a Huguenot name, though not a common one and, as is apt to happen in ancient records, spelt in various forms. There is also the difficulty that Scotland, unlike England, did not require the Huguenot refugees to register as 'stranger'. Finally, the imperfect state of the Scottish parochial registers would make it well nigh impossible to trace the family tree of a foreigner arriving at Inchinnan in 1560 or thereabouts to the simple weaver who went from the Kilbarchan district to Port Glasgow in 1792.

It is a fascinating puzzle, and the tradition of the family's Huguenot origin cannot be ruled out. It is simple historical fact that the Protestant refugees were welcomed to Scotland for their traditional skill in weaving. It is also relevant that Henry Birkmyre went to Port Glasgow as a weaver, to assist in the production of sailcloth, and not as a ropespinner.

Weaving was a staple village industry over wide areas of West Scotland before the processes of centralisation and mechanisation got to work. To this day one may come across in quite remote parts the shards of derelict small mills and rows of what were once workers' cottages. The trade was followed in the three large Renfrewshire villages of Inchinnan, Kilbarchan and Lochwinnoch—as well as in the county town of Paisley—and spilled over into Ayrshire. What can now be traced with certainty is a high incidence of Birkmyres in Kilbarchan in particular, that picturesque townlet still wrapped in charm and tradition despite the modernistic pressures about it.

The parish records witness to the marriages of three Birkmyres during the sixth decade of the 18th century—a Henry, a John and another John, the last specifically described as 'Weaver in Kilbarchan'. All married girls with good local names—Janet Craig, Agnes Carruth and Marion Hare. Of such folk was born the first Henry Birkmyre of The Gourock Ropework Company. He was born to Henry Birkmyre and his wife, Jane Craig, on January 12th, 1762. Only nine months previously Marion Hare, the wife of John Birkmyre, had given birth to a daughter christened Agnes. Young Henry and Agnes—full cousins and the bride older than her groom—were married in 1785. The first Family Bible states that young Henry was born in Lochwinnoch, and this may well have been so. Lochwinnoch and Kilbarchan are only five miles apart, and an honest weaver took employment where he could find it. It is still beyond a doubt that the young people who migrated to Port Glasgow in 1792 came thence from Kilbarchan and regarded it as their native place.

A portrait of the old gentleman—reproduced at the beginning of this chapter—has survived and hangs in the Board Room at Port Glasgow. It is not a major work of art, and his younger descendants are apt to be irreverent in their interpretations of the subject's aspect. The picture is nevertheless a fair enough likeness of a man with a candid, bland expression—the fact of a simple, honest sort of man. The hair over the forehead straggles in a curiously unkempt fashion, but underneath those untidy locks there gleams a shrewd pair of eyes, of such a colour and setting as detached observers see persisting in his descendants to this day.

The first Henry Birkmyre died on the first day of May 1844, and what is labelled as the 'Sederunt Book of the Estate of the late H. Birkmyre' has survived. The total value of the estate seems to have been in the region of £6,000, but it is made clear that he had already made substantial gifts to his sons, John and William. It then emerges that this John was an invalid 'from bodily indisposition incapable of acting or even of signifying whether he accepts or declines the office of Trustee' —the only other hint being that he had settled in business in Glasgow. He thus disappears completely from the record, the only other implication in the papers being that he died young.

To his wife the first Henry Birkmyre left an annual income of £150, substantial in the terms of the period; and she had been born a woman of what were then called the working classes. It is equally clear that his daughters had married men in relatively humble positions. The younger, Jean, had wed one, John Boyd, and the implication of the will is that he had deserted her. The elder daughter, Agnes, had found a husband in James Knox, wright in Port Glasgow, a wright being a joiner or a small builder at the most. To each of the girls he left £800, again a tidy sum in modern terms. The signatures of both of them to various docquets suggest elementary standards of education.

Some of the later entries in the Sederunt Book of Henry Birkmyre's estate throw odd little shafts of light on one aspect of life in that period. The weaving folk of those upland villages were a pious breed, often contentiously so, and the Birkmyres were firm Seceders, that is, they adhered to one of the many sects that broke away from the Church of Scotland during the ferment of the 18th century, often enough on very small points of doctrine. Thus, after her husband's death, we find Agnes Birkmyre asking the trustees for advances on her inheritance in order that she might benefit a Secession congregation in Port Glasgow. One of her grandsons, a Knox, definitely became a minister, while a younger brother also applied for an advance on his expectations to 'see him through College'—presumably to finance a course in Divinity at Glasgow University, then the old College in the High Street. It appears that William Birkmyre financed these improving schemes out of his own pocket and was duly reimbursed when the estate came to be wound up.

The financial niceties of the settlement, however, are irrelevant here. It is of more interest to us who know what was to happen later on that David Johnstone, appointed a trustee in Henry Birkmyre's will,

Henry II.

declined to accept the office. It is also of mild historical interest that the will was drawn up by John Patten, Writer to the Signet in Greenock, and that this name survives in the style of a legal firm still flourishing in that town. It is most important of all that William, old Henry Birkmyre's youngest child, was left in 1845 in a solid, if not yet commanding, position within The Gourock Ropework Company.

Only a few months after his father's death he was allowed, in terms of the copartnery he had entered in 1839, to take up his parent's share in The Gourock Ropework Company. In that year its funds were reckoned at £105,306 13s. 10d. The dividend on the share was £1,740 8s. 3d. William was now writing the minutes of the annual meeting of partners and, with a few inevitable fluctuations from year to year, could report steady progress until, in 1859, on the eve of his retirement, he could disburse dividends running up to nearly £6,000 each in value.

One uses the phrase 'running up', for by now the partners' holdings had been sub-divided by a variety of circumstances. There is no need to go into these in detail, nor into the financial movements whereby the sub-divisions were gathered together again into just three groups of holdings. In this respect the years 1843 and 1844 were vital.

The minutes of the 1843 meeting were the last signed by both Archibald Baine and the first Henry Birkmyre, and the handwriting in both cases is of old men very near the end. Indeed, they died within a few months of each other. In September 1843, a special meeting appointed William Birkmyre 'to assume the management of the concern' in place of Archibald Baine, now described for the first time as 'Managing Partner'. Baine's shares were therefore taken over by the surviving partners, and the appropriate minute, dated October 20th, 1843, was the last document signed by Henry Birkmyre I. For many years thereafter the minutes were signed by only three persons—Colin Campbell, David Johnstone and William Birkmyre. Later on, the signature of Henry II, William's oldest brother, is appended. He had inherited a small share in the company from his father and had taken over the management of its properties in Greenock, but his interest in the large affairs of the company was evanescent and unimportant.

Through the confusion of years of change in these financial matters a clear picture of the standing of the partners emerges only with the minutes for 1853, a new contract among them being then necessary. By this it was agreed that Colin Campbell held 28/100th of the capital (the stock valued at £60,000), Colin Campbell, Jr., 24/100th, William Birkmyre 28/100th, David Johnstone 16/100th and Henry Birkmyre 4/100th. Colin Campbell, Sr., was a non-active partner in the concern and could afford to keep up a handsome estate in Dunbartonshire, just across the Clyde from Port Glasgow. This Campbell holding had been inherited, passed down from partners in the original Campbells, Lee and Company. The father and son of that name therefore dominated the finances of The Gourock Ropework Company with their majority holding, even if Johnstone and the Birkmyres were doing all the work.

The Campbells retain an interest in The Gourock to this day, and Sir Jock Campbell acted as a Director for a period until the pressure of his own interests in London rendered the long journeys to the North inconvenient.

An early view of Port Glasgow, done in colour by J. Clark in 1820, gives quite fantastic prominence in the scene to the works of The Gourock Ropework Company. These are shown as a sort of gigantic barracks on the present site near Newark Castle. The sketch was made in a romantic age, and we may take the obvious exaggeration and even the placing of the building, as little bits of artistic licence. On the other hand, a plan of the town drawn in 1799 suggests a site farther west, nearer the existing railway station and the original ropewalk, still in productive use, is shown to run some 400 yards from that point eastwards. Unfortunately, Archibald Baine's minutes of the annual meetings are sparing of geographical detail, and how the Company's premises were disposed about Port Glasgow in the early years of the 19th century must be largely guesswork.

It has been shown that the partners acquired a cotton and barley mill in 1800, but surely not for carrying on these trades. We know that the Spinning Mill and its steam engine were set up in 1805; and that may be the large building shown in Clark's print. Then there appear in the accounts as assets such as in 1819, New Warehouse, and not a hint as to where it is situated. Later on there appear with equal vagueness, such items as New Drying House, Workmen's Houses and (most mysteriously) Milliken & Wellington Warehouse. Two major developments are quite clearly accounted for, however.

In 1841, while the first Henry Birkmyre was still alive and his son, William, the very active manager of the firm, the company set up in

Greenock, on the Shaws Water, an establishment of some magnitude. Known locally as The Cut, the Shaws Water scheme was a bold adventure by the magistrates of Greenock to carry the surplus water from their reservoir behind the hills above the town round the western buttress of the high moorland country; that is, instead of cutting a tunnel expensively through hard igneous rock. The Cut is still a favourite walk, commanding splendid views of the Firth of Clyde, but the purpose of Shaws Water was purely functional. From its terminal, near the existing Upper Greenock Station on the Wemyss Bay line, at the foot of what is called the Whinhill, it was to—and it still does—supply water power to industrial establishments along a line of falls from the high ground to the sea. Up here The Gourock Ropework Company elected in 1841 to set up a mill and ropewalk.

The value of this property remained for many years the largest single asset in the Company's books. But the tendency was towards the centralisation of the manufacturing processes about Port Glasgow. By 1845, for example, a 'New Ropework for renewing old Ropework' had been built there. The minute of June 11th, 1856, declares:—

'It having been suggested to the Partners that it would be an improvement to the business if all the sailcloth yarns which are required for the manufacture of their sailcloth could be spun in Port Glasgow. This would tend to condense the sailcloth manufacture more and at the same time save the expense of the carriage of the yarn. This, of course, would leave the Greenock Mill idle, and it is suggested that, in order to employ it, to employ it in the spinning and manufacture of Jute Goods'.

It will be observed that the good William Birkmyre was hardly a master of elegant prose, but his recommendations went through. These included the increase of steam power in the main Port Glasgow mill to just short of 100 b.h.p., the provision of machinery for dealing with jute, and the necessary apparatus for spinning. The partners put an upper limit of £8,000 on the expenditure involved.

The experiment with jute at the Greenock mill was apparently not a great success. In 1860 the mill was sold, though the ropewalk was retained for a time. In 1862 the partners agreed that, 'in consequence of the increase of business and extension of our works', the capital stock of the Company should be raised from £60,000 to £90,000. They were doing very well in those years, the assets as recorded in the accounts of 1862 amounting to £231,305; and one notes that, apart from the large

John I—John Birkmyre of Broadstone and his wife.

stock of goods held in the Greenock warehouse, there were large accumulations in Glasgow and Liverpool as well. In 1868 it was agreed that 'the manufacture of the Company's goods would henceforth be carried on solely at Port Glasgow'.

To this end the partners laid out considerable sums of money on the acquisition of land and the purchase of existing property. They bought, for instance, for £14,000, the sugar refinery of Messrs. James Richardson & Co. 'at the east end of Port Glasgow', and another reference describes this building as being in or at Newark. This suggests that the hard core of old Port Glasgow was about the harbour and Custom-house, and that the hamlet of Newark was regarded as a sort of suburb, near the castle already described. This was the building that, inevitably altered from time to time, has become the nexus of the Company's operations today. It is a landmark, a rather gaunt factory in red brick, the central block seven storeys high, that seems to close the approach to Port Glasgow from the east and forces road traffic to turn sharp right and then left to gain the main road from the Port to Gourock through the long length of Greenock.

By this time, however, William Birkmyre was dead. The first Colin Campbell followed him to the grave within a year or two. And thus was set the scene in which members of the third generation of Birkmyres were to play leading parts in the affairs of The Gourock Ropework Company during the last four decades of the 19th century.

As it was in 1837, the old East Harbour of Port Glasgow with its lock-gate still in position. Although still in use, it is destined to be filled in to give access for the new East-West main road. When it is filled in, the oldest dry dock in Scotland, located at the west end of the harbour, will cease to exist.

Chapter IV

YEARS OF EXPANSION

The first William Birkmyre had six children. The oldest was a daughter, Agnes, who distinguished herself in due course by bearing 13 children. The youngest was a boy, Archibald, who preferred scholarship to industry and studied for the Church, becoming at length minister of Kinning Park Free Church in Glasgow, a south side charge in which he laboured until 1880 when he retired.

His labours there had a curious consequence. Often enough in the old days the Port Glasgow office received letters, enquiring as to the provenance of the unusual name Birkmyre, the writers declaring it to be included among the Christian names of themselves or relations. This was latterly explained by the fact that, according to a custom of the period, parents of children being brought forward for baptism might

45

minority at this stage, their joint holding only a trifle larger than that of Johnstone alone, but the situation was to change completely before many years had passed.

Intermittently, the partners considered at their annual meeting the position of the sons of partners on the death of the latter. This was never decisively settled. A typical minute, for August 1867, left the question in the air, thus: 'Nothing is decided, but the son or sons of such deceasing partners are recommended to the favourable consideration of the surviving partners, with a view, if circumstances will permit, of them being admitted as partners and enjoying a portion of the share his father held'. The legal bearing of this conclusion was as imprecise as the grammar in which it is expressed, and it led to difficulties in due course.

While David Johnstone lived he was undoubtedly manager by appointment, with Henry and John Birkmyre as his assistants. All three, however, were on the same salary scale of £400 a year, and this suggests that the distinction of grades was nominal. (After all, the works expanding in both Port Glasgow and Greenock, and so many different processes being employed, each could have his own large share of responsibility.) If there were any personal feelings at work within the triangle of responsibility, these are naturally not reflected in the minutes, and there is no reason to fancy that jealousies had formed about the scene. When David Johnstone died in 1880, however, the conflict inherent in the loose agreement about the rights of partners' sons began to take shape.

David Johnstone had a son, David Edward, who had been in New Zealand, but was by this time, April 29th, 1880, coming home to claim his patrimony. At the same time, Henry Birkmyre II claimed the right to have his own son—a third William—admitted to the copartnery and to transfer to the young man a moiety of his own shares in the concern. This was all arranged without any apparent disagreement, and both young men were duly assumed into the copartnery and both authorised to sign for the firm. But the youngest Birkmyre had a strong father and a solid uncle behind him, while David Edward Johnstone seems to have stood alone. In this dramatic grouping Colin Campbell appears to have stood apart, well content with excellent dividends.

David Edward Johnstone did not long survive as a partner in The Gourock Ropework Company. There are now no means of knowing if personalities were involved in the breach; it is merely obvious that, coming into the business late, he could not stand up against the long

John II—'John Junior'.

experience of the Birkmyres. However that may be, he made at the annual meeting on May 17th, 1884, a declaration that must have sounded strangely dramatic in the office at Port Glasgow. It is minuted thus:—

'As the contract of copartnery terminated on tenth May last and as D. Edward Johnstone retires from the business at that date, the manager is instructed to pay him the amount of his stock less the sum standing at the debit of his account current. . . .'

'D. Edward Johnstone stated at the commencement of the meeting, and shortly after retired from same, that his presence was to be held as not acquiescing or concurring in any resolutions which were passed'.

Once again, we cannot now know with certainty what was the inwardness of the dispute. Since the minute was signed by the largest individual shareholder, Colin Campbell, it would almost seem that David Edward Johnstone had been found wanting and had been dismissed. The subsequent dispute between him and his late partners went to arbitration with Mr. J. Marshall Hill, a Glasgow solicitor, as oversman.

In the issue, as we shall see, the arbitrator awarded Johnstone the sum of £12,952 6s. 6d. in discharge of his claim—this compared with his nominal holding of nearly £24,000 in the books. And so ended the Johnstone connection with The Gourock. Colin Campbell, the second, died in February 1886, and his interest passed to his two sons, W. Middleton Campbell and Henry A. Campbell, but neither of these young men took any direct interest in the conduct of the business. In any case, they were now in the financial minority. According to the accounts of 1886, the various holdings were valued thus:—

W. Middleton Campbell	£27,000
Henry A. Campbell	27,000
Henry Birkmyre	47,250
John Birkmyre	47,250
William Birkmyre	13,500

On this total stock of £162,000 the partners agreed to pay themselves a dividend at the rate of 8 per cent. Henry Birkmyre signed the minute on mandate for his son, William, then travelling in Australia in the company's interest. The most significant feature of the entry, however, is that it shows the Birkmyre financial interests in The Gourock Ropework Company to have become as dominant as they had long been on the managerial side. The Campbells could continue to profit by inheritance.

During those last two decades of the 19th century the business of The Gourock was continually expanding geographically as well as in manufacturing power. The accounts for 1881 show that as much as £15,000 had been invested in the building or acquisition of workmen's houses. Warehouses in Liverpool and London had already been set up, as well as in Greenock and Glasgow, but now the range was being extended into Lowestoft, Yarmouth, Plymouth, Hull—the great centres of the English fishing industry. The Company, however obliquely, took an interest in the Grimsby and North Sea Steam Trawling Company Limited. The purchase of an office and warehouse at Cape Town is briefly mentioned in the minutes of the 1901 meeting. These also intimate, but with tantalising vagueness, that shares had been taken in a company set up to manufacture trawl twine at Grimsby.

The Gourock Ropework Company could never get far away from the sea on which its fortunes had been so largely based since the early 18th century, when the Firth of Clyde was alive with fishing craft, when Gourock was a busy fishing port, and when Greenock had as its first motto 'Let herring swim that trade maintain'. Towards the end of the 19th century there creeps into the accounts, always sparing of general information, an item curtly entered as 'Ships and Steamers', and the detached reader's first impression is that the Company required a small fleet of vessels to carry its products hither and thither. Another curt entry in the appropriate minutes explains that the partners had decided to buy shares in established shipping concerns that would come to The Gourock for their needs in cordage and canvas. In one year towards the turn of the century the investment under this head was put as high as £40,000.

At the same time, extension of the Company's manufacturing potential on shore had been put in hand. The minutes of the 1898 meeting record the decision to purchase for the modest sum of £2,100 a property in Lynedoch Street, Greenock. This building, though much altered, is still one of the Company's productive units. The intention was to equip it for the manufacture of binder twine, then coming into increasing demand with the introduction of the self-binding reaping machine from the States. This establishment was deliberately set up in the larger neighbouring town, not far from the ropework on the Shaws Water, for

John III—'Young John'.

52

the duly minuted reason—'female labour being scarce in Port Glasgow and plentiful in Greenock'. It did not, in fact, go immediately into production of binder twine. As we shall see later on, its first task was a strange one indeed.

But towards this end of the 19th century the men of the third Birkmyre generation were ageing. The sons of the first William Birkmyre—Henry II and John—had carried the load of increasing responsibility for many years; and it should again be emphasised that from the days of the original Henry, the foreman promoted partner, to this present hour of writing, The Gourock Ropework Company has never been without a Birkmyre in immediate daily charge of its affairs.

The first of the third Birkmyre generation to go was Henry II. He began to ail in the mid 1890's and remained a sick man until his death on May 4th, 1900; his brother William, former M.P. for Ayr Burghs, having predeceased him by only a fortnight. In any view of the Birkmyre achievement as a whole Henry II stands out as the prime consolidator of the business his father, William I, had so brilliantly expanded. The first Henry had been a man of the 18th century; the first William had spanned two centuries; the second Henry was all Victorian solidity, the bluff, red-bearded figure shown in the portrait that hangs in the Board Room at Port Glasgow.

The outline of his career is perfectly in the Victorian pattern. Over and above his large and complex business interests he took in his stride all his obligations as a local magnate. Like his father before him, he became a member of Port Glasgow Town Council and duly served as Provost of the burgh. His term of office over, he was elected to the local School Board and acted as chairman of that body for three years. Henry Birkmyre II was likewise in character as a Victorian merchant of the old school in being a staunch churchman; founder of the Clune Park United Presbyterian Church and its presiding genius, under the minister, until his death.

The United Presbyterians were a large denomination outwith the Church of Scotland proper, but various unions brought the bulk of them back into the Auld Kirk, and what was the Clune Park U.P. Church is now within the national fold. Henry Birkmyre started as a Liberal of the old school, but he split with the Gladstonians on the Irish Home Rule issue and ended his long and useful life as what used to be called a Unionist.

Alexander Brander Allan.

His brother John was a man of equal solidity, if perhaps without the drive and lasting power of his senior. He was unusual among the Birkmyres of that generation in being childless. Henry II, on the other hand, was twice married and fathered a large family—12 in all. There were many girls among them, and some of the sons played no part in the conduct of the business.

The youngest, Archibald, was sent to Calcutta and there established the Hastings Mills, managed by the firm of Birkmyre Brothers. This Archibald did well in India, playing his part in political as well as business affairs, and he was honoured with a baronetcy in due course, but that aspect of the Birkmyre saga hardly concerns us. At home in Port Glasgow the management of the parent firm had passed to three of his brothers—William III, James and John; the last invariably known as John Birkmyre, Jr., to distinguish him from his uncle of Broadstone. The appropriate minute of May 17th, 1895, indicates the resignation from active management of Henry II and John I in that year, for Henry was by now a sick man and John inclined to take life easy.

The three younger men kept the flag flying briskly over a number of years, but it is clear that their father's death called for a revision of the basic financial position. Over and above his large interest in The Gourock Ropework Company proper, Henry II invested his private fortune, as at Calcutta, in other ventures of a similar nature. The most important of these—the cotton mills at New Lanark—was brought into the orbit of The Gourock by an agreement made on October 15th, 1903, whereby the incorporation of the Company as a limited liability concern was prepared for.

All surviving partners signed on behalf of the old private company, John Birkmyre of Broadstone, William Middleton Campbell of Colgrain, Henry A. Campbell now living in Norfolk, and Henry II's three sons; William, James and John, Jr. The document foreshadowed the incorporation of The Gourock Ropework Company Limited, with a nominal capital of £720,000, divided into 360,000 five per cent Cumulative Preference Shares of £1 each and 360,000 Ordinary Shares of £1 each. The significant clause in the Agreement, however, is that which runs thus:—'Whereas . . . certain of the vendors have for some years carried on business at New Lanark as manufacturers of Doubled Cotton Yarns and Fishing Nets, which latter business, with the whole property and assets thereof, has recently been acquired by the Vendors . . .'

Thus the copartnery that started modestly enough to make ropes on on the shores of Gourock Bay in the 18th century was absorbing another concern with a strange, and indeed romantic, history. This was the first major expansion beyond the Gourock–Greenock–Port Glasgow district.

The story of New Lanark is a fascinating one, and it will be outlined later on. The controlling power was still in Port Glasgow, however, and the mill there remained, and remains, the most productive unit of the expanding business.

*The present Board of Directors and Secretary of The Gourock Ropework Co. Ltd:
left to right: Henry Birkmyre Semple (son of the Chairman); John Fullarton Birkmyre
('Mr Ian'), Sales Director and Deputy Chairman; John Maxwell, W.S.; Commander
Hugh Egerton Semple, R.N. (Retd.), Chairman and Managing Director and Deputy
Lieutenant of the County of Renfrew; R. I. Campbell, Secretary; David Lumsden
Morgan, Production Director. In the background Robert Owen's portrait looks down.*

57

Chapter V

ON THE HUMAN SIDE

The preponderance of female labour employed by The Gourock Ropework Company is one of the striking features of this type of factory work. There must always be a proportion of men on the engineering and maintenance sides, in the supervisory grades, and for hard and skilled labour in the ropewalks. But the spinning frames and the looms need the nimble-fingered, patient girls to serve them, and it is in Port Glasgow as in the cotton towns of Lancashire; the mill-girl has been for long the queen of the local labour market. That girl went early to work 'in the mill', daughter succeeding mother, perhaps learning from her, through generation after generation. The wealth of experience involved in this industrial sequence would set up a regional novelist for life.

Fortunately, a few years ago, somebody within the organisation at Port Glasgow had the excellent idea of collecting reminiscences from retired workers. Most of these people were very old, some illiterate, and some hazy as to the details of their working lives, but, apart from the few who could put their memories on paper, the work was done by interview or tape-recording, so that we have preserved for us a *corpus* of testimony that illuminates the nature of labouring life within the Mill as far back as 1880. Most of the witnesses inevitably talk from limited experience within a niche of a vast manufactory, but the mass of reminiscence breaks down easily into a set of fixed themes.

One of Mr Fyfe's contemporaries fortunately provided the material of a sketch of the office arrangements at Port Glasgow in those quieter days. Mr D. McTaggart became an office boy in 1904 under the then chief clerk, Mr John Sinclair. He tells us that Sinclair always wore a tail coat in navy blue and, through the working day had perched on his head a small cap, like a schoolboy's, in lustre. This was a man of economical habit. He carefully slit open all the incoming envelopes, and on the blank sides of these wrote out the Works orders for the day, delivering them in person to the departments concerned. The firm's

59

letters were all written by hand and copied in a hand press. A Blick typewriter was installed in 1904 and 'treated like a bomb'. One telephone in a booth outside the outer office served the business for many a long day.

Charles McPhee, who later provides the reminiscences of the outing to Carse, could go further back in time, having started in 1889 as office and store boy, though he latterly became an operative. He worked from 8.30 in the morning until 7.30 in the evening as a rule, and one of his first morning tasks was to carry in a supply of dross for the two coal fires, one in the outer office, one in the partners' room behind, in which each of the Birkmyre brothers of the third generation—he was careful to explain in a curious phrase—'had a chair of his own'. He added that, as a mere child of 13-plus, he went once a fortnight to the bank some distance away to draw money for the wages of the whole mill. From the first outing he returned with two sealed bags: gold and silver in one, paper money in the other. The second trip was for coppers.

John Fyfe's reminiscences complete this picture of the past with two nice 'period' touches. During the Spanish-American War of 1898 supplies of manila from the Philippines were interrupted and prices rose steeply, changing sometimes three times a week. Head Office then had to advise all branches and the principal customers in the United Kingdom of these fluctuations, and this meant the issue of some 700 circulars at a time. As office boy, Fyfe was obliged to write all labels by hand, laboriously copying from the address book. And on most nights of the working week, crisis or no crisis, he had to run to the Post Office to catch the 7.45 p.m. mail.

One of those pensioners of The Gourock interviewed before it was too late, Mr John Fyfe (who started work in 1898), was able to provide a list of stores supplied to an average sailing ship before the days of wire ropes. He insisted that his figures were approximate, but they are interesting, thus:—

> 5 tons manila ropes
> 2-3 tons bolt-rope and cordage.
> One-half ton boat-lacing, etc.
> 60-70 pieces sailcloth.
> 5 cwts. sail-twine for sewing.

He added that among the regular customers of the period were the Allan Line, the City Line, Burrell & Sons, Maclay & McIntyre, and the Hogarth Line: all large shipowners when Glasgow was a busier shipowning port than it is today. Mr Fyfe also told of very large export orders regularly despatched from Port Glasgow—50-60 tons of rope at a time to Buenos Aires or to Antipodean ports for the use of the New Zealand Steamship Company; Birkmyre's Cloth to South America and India in any quantity from 50 to 100 bales in one shipment; wagon covers made up for the South American railways then being constructed and 'Ferrocaril tents' for native workmen on those adventurous lines.

There is a strange pathos in some of these memories, especially as the old folk compare the conditions in which they worked with those enjoyed by their successors to-day. Mrs Kate Kinney started in the mill, a barefooted girl, on her 14th birthday, March 1st, 1888. She remembered the dry closets, the shortage of drinking water, and the indifferent light of gas in fish-tail burners.

. . . This gas-lighting business seems to have left a curiously strong impression on those workers of 70 years or so ago. One very old witness —the tape-recording sadly revealing the failure of his powers and the thickness of his Clydeside speech—was almost vehement on the subject.

'Aye,' he declared, 'there was gas all over. There was an old man they called Jimmy Seals came in every morning and lit them'. He then explained that several entrances to the mill had to be left open and went on: 'Well, on a coarse morning, you know how the wind blows. The gas went straight out, and you could hardly see anything. Then on the winter mornings, with frost and snow, the pipes were frozen, and there we waited till daylight'.

One trusts that the supply of gas was cut off at the main in these circumstances. This old fellow could not recall when electricity was laid on for lighting. He could only aver that 'It was in Jimmy Bonnar's time,' adding, 'I was feart whenever the electric light cam' on'. He was afraid whenever the electric lights were switched on.

For all the workers the day started at 6 a.m. and finished at 5.30 p.m. with two breaks for breakfast and dinner of three-quarters of an hour each. But there was no works canteen in those days, and these breaks must have been crowded for many of the girls. As a beginner Mrs Kinney received 3s. 6d. a week, paid fortnightly, and she makes the point—repeated in other testimonies—that The Gourock's management would have nothing to do with the 'quartering' system: that is, a

Typical of the 'Old School' of workers, Kate Kinney as she was just before her retirement.

small deduction of wage for bad timekeeping. The laggard was sent home and told to come back after the dinner hour.

In the event, Mrs Kinney was dismissed for a breach of factory discipline. At the age of 57, after 43 years of service, she was discovered cleaning her machines as they were being 'run out': that is, still in motion. Some pundit in the general office decreed that there was no pay due to her, still less a pension, and she appealed through the Works Manager, a Mr Sangster, who, she later declared 'should be in Heaven'. This Sangster got her a 'single-end' dwelling in the block of workers' flats the Company had built along the southern edge of their rambling property; and as her family came along, Mrs Kinney got a room and kitchen flat, apparently rent free. During the Second World War, at the age of 69, she returned to the mill and did her daily stint in what she called 'the Arcade'.

It will be agreed that Mrs Kinney must have been a woman of character, and though the conditions of her early employment in Victorian times were admittedly drab, she could look on the bright side. For her the Birkmyres were 'good masters'. Discussing her apparently low rate of wages, she could point out details of the relatively low cost of living—sugar at 2d. per lb., tea at 2s. per lb., milk at 1d. per pint. Male contributors to the symposium feelingly recalled that a bottle of Guinness cost 2d. and a five-gill bottle of the best whisky 3s. 6d.

One of these was James Starrett, who was 12½ years old when he started work in 1891, receiving 2s. 6d. a week, paid fortnightly. Over 50 years later he was to be awarded the B.E.M. for outstanding service. This male witness contributed a curious note of feminine interest. Apparently some of the women workers came from Greenock. Then he offered the alarming information that these young women, rising at 4 a.m. at the latest, gathered in the central square of Greenock and marched—singing—to their work in Port Glasgow, a distance of more than three miles. He added that they *might* be lucky enough to get a horse bus home at night.

In much the same context another male witness contributed a fashion note of some oddity. Most women workers of that distant period wore the traditional garb of their kind—shawls that could be drawn over their heads in wet weather, even used to hammock an infant. It appears, however, that the girls in the Sail Loft, enjoying better pay than their sisters, wore bonnets and white starched blouses as the badge of their superiority.

On the masculine side, however, 'the Greenock hecklers' (the men who hackled the raw flax and hemp by hand—a heavy and wearying task) enjoyed the strange privilege of having one of their number read aloud from a newspaper or novel as they worked. The newspaper, the

63

evidence runs, was invariably *The Glasgow Herald*. Lord Beaverbrook had not then swung into action.

One has to imagine the lives of all these people dominated by the mill bell—'the surly, sullen bell' of the poet's fancy. Birkmyre's bell, so to call it, also served as the town's bell of the burgh of Port Glasgow. One veteran recalled that one of his treats as a child was to be allowed to stay up to hear this bell ring in the New Year, then the most important of the Scottish festivals. This instrument was cast in Greenock by the old firm of James Duff & Company, and one of the veterans assures us that Henry and John Birkmyre, the sons of the great William, cast coins into the melt in the traditional way. On working mornings it started ringing at 5.30 a.m., and this was the job of one whose surname is vaguely, but not with certainty, remembered to be Simpson.

One Saturday night this worthy treated himself well in the public houses of Port Glasgow. Having fallen into a heavy sleep, he was awakened next morning by the alarum clock that works in the subconscious of most of us and, the feeling of guilt no doubt heavy upon him, hurried to the mill and started to agitate the rope. Thus the decent people of Port Glasgow had their precious slumber broken at 5.30 a.m. on a Sunday morning.

The works at Port Glasgow are nowadays powered by electricity, of course, but it is interesting that many of the male pensioners reminisced in detail about the steam engines that used to drive the machines. They were all children of the Victorian age, and a large steam engine took on for them something of the character of a tribal image. One or two of the very old men could recall a period when the ropewalk at least was powered by a beam engine, no doubt a clumsy, cranky piece of machinery. The sentimental affection of the majority was for 'Jane', thus quite solemnly christened, as a brass plate in the board room testifies to this day. Again according to Victorian custom, this engine, like a ship, was named after Jane Fullarton, daughter of a Provost of Greenock and wife of John Birkmyre II. It is perhaps of little interest now that 'The Jane', as the engine was always affectionately known among the workers, was a horizontal compound job of 250 b.h.p., driving the machinery in two flats and taking also some auxiliary loads. It is perhaps more remarkable that her memory is cherished as that of an Ancient Monument.

Starrett, B.E.M., Master Ropemaker, photographed at work on one of the ropes for 'Mayflower II'. He was called back from retirement ... job which demanded highly specialised knowledge and experience and the employment of certain techniques which only he could remember.

... of Old Port Glasgow showing the 'Brick Building' in the background with the Mill bell which had to be removed when part of the roof was destroyed by fire.

Not a photograph of the Board and Managers of the Company as you might think but our earliest record of the staff of the Mechanic Shop whose task it was, amongst other things, to nurse mighty engines such as the 1,500 h.p. beam engine shown opposite.

The not inconsiderable muscle of 'Jane' was augmented by—one had almost said married to—a larger engine in 1907. This was a machine of 500 b.h.p., always called 'The Greenock', because it had first been installed in the Lynedoch Street premises to cope, as we shall see, with the heavy demand for tents during the South African War. It could be coupled with 'Jane' to take especially heavy loads. Another maker's nameplate in the Board Room commemorates a large beam engine of 1,500 b.h.p. in the main engine-house that did the most yeoman service of all. For 75 years and with only *two* minor stoppages, this huge engine, as high as a three-storey building, drove the bulk of the Mill machinery by multiple ropeband drive from the 80-foot circumference 80-ton flywheel.

With only two minor breakdowns this massive beam engine for seventy-five years drove most of the Port Glasgow Works. It was as high as a three-storey building and could not, therefore, be photographed as a unit. This artist's impression may give some idea of its size, bearing in mind that the flywheel was over 80 feet in circumference and weighed over 80 tons.

There is much in those reminiscences of the past one would be happy to dwell on, but one theme is recurrent. It reveals the existence within The Gourock in those days of a strong sense of community under the benevolent patriarchy of the Birkmyres. Charles McPhee, earlier mentioned, was of a large family who all worked in the mill—nine brothers, three sisters and, latterly, three sons. The workers were never left with any sense of a remote directorate. The Birkmyre partners, fathers and sons, uncles and nephews, were always about, often enough lending a hand with the job of production in an emergency.

The perfect expression of this family feeling, so to call it, was the occasional works outing. Most of the witnesses interviewed a few years ago referred to this treat, this great day of escape from hard work and the rather dark little township under the Renfrewshire hills. Nowadays, an expedition of the sort would be an affair of motor-coaches, paper streamers and organised catering. Fifty years ago and more the workers were entertained to a sail in one of the numerous Clyde river steamers of those days and transported to some spot on the Clyde coast where a games field was available. The simple provisions and instruments of the feast—tea urns, drums of milk, meat pies, sandwiches, pastries and the rest—were carried with the expedition. At least one Birkmyre and his lady accompanied the large party.

Charles McPhee, again, testified that 'the whole mill went from the Mirren Shore by steamer' to Carse. (The Mirren Shore is still the regional name for the Port Glasgow harbour area.) Carse is a small estate in Western Argyll, then occupied by John Birkmyre, Jr., and it is said that this outing celebrated his marriage to Jane Fullarton. One merely observes that the task of transporting a horde of mill workers by steamboat to Tarbert, Lochfyne, getting them over to the Atlantic shore by horse-drawn brake and home again was a considerable feat of logistics. At Carse, McPhee got the curious impression that the whole field was 'covered with milk cans'. He then added that this first excursion, when he was only 14, took place on a Friday, and that foot-racing and football were among the diversions of the day. He also added a curious phrase to the effect that 'both religions' took part in the sports.

This is a somewhat sinister echo of an old conflict that is now, happily, calming down. It was the conflict between the native Scot and the immigrant Irish, between the Presbyterian and the Catholic. It still conditions life on industrial Clydeside to some extent. There is never-

*This is **The Gourock** First Eleven of 1908/9 (they didn't have a second eleven at that time). **Only one member** of this team, Mr David Lindgreen, Chief Cashier at Head Office, and fifth from right in the photograph, is still in the active service of the Company. He recollects that this photograph was taken on the occasion of the annual 'needle' match with Langbank and that The Gourock won.*

theless much historical interest in the fact that an old man, interviewed in 1954, could trot out this fact as a memorable feature of an outing in 1902.

The best word on this subject—and, as befits a female witness—was provided by Mrs Kate Kinney. She could recall a day in 1888 when the workers were taken by steamer up the Clyde to Glasgow to visit the Exhibition of that year. Each girl carried a flag, and three bands—of the local Volunteer Artillery, St John's and the Salvation Army—accompanied them. 'There was no work in the shipyards that morning, what with the men watching the mill girls leaving,' she testified; and she quoted a local parody of an old song, 'Wha' wadna' fecht for Charlie?', thus:—

> Wha saw Birkmyres, the workers?
> Wha saw them gang awa'?
> Wha saw Birkmyres, the workers?
> Sailing to the Broomielaw?

'It was a great day,' concluded Mrs Kinney, 'the best we ever had'. It must have been a formidable affair indeed. A male witness of the same period declares that there were then between 1,700 and 1,800 workers in the mill, and that they took half an hour 'to skail'—that is, to disperse after working hours.

What manner of men were these early Birkmyres, employers of so much local labour in a highly specialised trade? The men of the third generation—Henry II, John of Broadstone, James, William the M.P. for Ayr Burghs, and Adam—are all documented, so to speak, in one way or another. The first Henry and his able son, William, except in so far as the portrait of the older man in the Back Office at Port Glasgow suggests a shrewd but modest personality, elude our understanding.

Some surmises as to the nature of these men are permissible and probably valid, however. The first Henry Birkmyre was a plain weaver from the uplands of Renfrewshire, and we may be sure that his speech was of the country sort, good 'braid Scots' without frills. On the other hand, the Scottish parish school of his period invariably provided a sound grounding in the three R's, and old Henry's handwriting is clear if hardly stylish. It is an interesting fact that the handwriting of his son William is much of the same character, and it is a reasonable surmise that the boy was educated in Port Glasgow in the traditional way, with perhaps a little polish applied at some regional grammar school.

Father and son were both God-fearing men, pillars of their chosen kirk; and William did his communal duty on the local Town Council. That they were able and industrious in their business affairs hardly needs saying. In short, it is legitimate to see these two Birkmyres of the first two generations as keen business men of their period, content with their small world in the Clydeside town, even if the goods they produced were travelling all over the globe.

There still stand beside the main office block of The Gourock Ropework Company in Bay Street, Port Glasgow, two old houses in a decent tradition of domestic architecture. The passer-by might recognise them as good old dwellings that have seen better days, defeated as residences by the heavy traffic surging up and down the main road to and from Greenock. (Small flats of them are still occupied into the 1960's by a few pensioners and such, but the houses are scheduled to be taken over eventually for works extensions when tenants' rights expire.) One of these dwellings was for many years the town house of the Birkmyre family, the executive partners living beside their place of work. It was abandoned as such only towards the end of the 19th century, as we shall see. In the meantime, the brothers in the third generation began to move to the more agreeable quarters their success in business fully justified.

It appears that Henry II took the first step outside the town, perhaps because his family was a large one, building the solid house called 'Springbank' on a bluff overlooking the ship-channel of the Clyde. The move was not a dramatic one in terms of distance. Springbank can be reached in a ten-minute walk eastwards from the Mill, as it was called in those days. It still stands, a square-fronted sort of small mansion, but it is thickly built about by workers' dwellings in the tenement style, and its function nowadays is of a social nature. In 1929 Sir James Lithgow of the shipbuilding firm, grandson of Henry Birkmyre II, bought and endowed it as a convalescent home for the sick children of Port Glasgow and district, the home to be administered by the Trustees of the Broadstone Jubilee Hospital, of which we shall hear more later on. It passed in 1947 into the care of the Church of Scotland, and in 1953, after a fire and with help from a provision in the will of Miss Jessie Birkmyre, another daughter of Henry Birkmyre II, it was dedicated as a Community Centre. To the confusion of historians the name was changed from Springbank to Sunnybank.

Springbank was an isolated sort of place when it was built, however, a proper home for a captain of local industry and the Provost of the town, and as such as it was a sort of ancestral seat of the Birkmyre dynasty for two generations on end. Interviewed in 1959, one or two veteran workers could recall Mr Henry coming from Springbank to the mill each morning in his carriage and pair, always with a spaniel gallumphing along with the horses. It is also on record that, when the weather was reasonably fair, Mr Henry invariably walked home for luncheon, often enjoying one restful half-hour of slumber thereafter. One day he turned up the steep drive leading to the house and was obliged to jump aside as a horseless carriage bore down upon him at speed. This was his own carriage, occupied only by his young son, John, who had wheeled the vehicle out of the coachhouse and set off down the drive to taste the delights of high-speed travel. This John was to become Chairman and Managing Director of The Gourock in due course and himself the occupant of Springbank for many years.

John, the brother of Henry II and uncle of the charioteer, moved still farther away from Port Glasgow, but only to a distance that seems negligible now. His wife, a Miss Maclarty, bore him no children, but she was apparently a managing sort of woman, and this couple expressed themselves in the creation of a small estate and mansionhouse much grander than Springbank. This was, and is, Broadstone, the estate having been created out of two adjoining parts of the old lands of Broadfield and Finlaystone. Again, on a bluff above the Clyde, Mr and Mrs John built their home in the Scots Baronial manner, surrounding it with expanses of lawn and a huge walled garden that required a small army of men to maintain them in their heyday. If this John Birkmyre had any eccentricities they were well under the control of his able wife. They travelled widely in Europe in their latter years, and some of the decorative features they admired abroad were built into the fabric of Broadstone and its approaches. But the mansionhouse has gone the way of so many places built by industrial wealth near populous places. It is now a unit of a specialised group within the Regional Hospitals Board.

It seems to have been Adam Birkmyre, the youngest of William I's sons, who led the way to what could fairly be called the creation of a Birkmyre colony in Kilmacolm—accent on the last syllable. This place was then a remote upland village, enjoying utterly unpolluted air at heights up to 500 feet above sea level and lying serenely in a basin of agricultural country on the edge of the Renfrewshire moorlands. The construction of the Glasgow & South Western Railway line to Princess Pier at Greenock connected it with Glasgow by a fairly frequent service, and soon the villas of the decently prosperous were going up over the fields and up the hill towards what is now an excellent golf course. Kilmacolm remains wholly residential, but still so near the country that you may see passing through it now and again the hounds, horses and pink coats of the Lanark and Renfrewshire Hunt.

Adam Birkmyre appears to have been early on this scene of development. On the south side of the village he built himself a substantial villa, giving it the fine Tennysonian name of 'Shallott'. More than that, though probably to secure his amenities, he bought a tidy bit of ground and gave it over to the local authority as a public park, and Birkmyre Park is a pleasant corner to this day. Other members of the family gravitated towards this agreeable place which, though still seemingly remote, is only about four or five miles by road from Port Glasgow.

Three active Directors of The Gourock, the Chairman included, live in Kilmacolm to this day, the journey downhill being a mere matter of minutes in a modern car. Shallot, like Springbank and Broadstone, however, has ceased to be a Birkmyre stronghold and is now a girls' school.

The youngest son of William Birkmyre I, Adam, was never formally admitted a partner in The Gourock Ropework Company. His business on its behalf was foreign travelling, and this duty took him over large expanses of the World's surface. When he was at home, and perhaps because he never married, he developed as an eccentric with some surprising foibles. He was apparently so much afraid of draughts that he persuaded a firm of coachbuilders to fabricate a hansom cab of which the passenger seat looked backwards. In the same vein he had a revolving summer house built in his garden and, when he chose to occupy it, one of his butler's duties was to come out and turn this contraption so that the master could have the benefit of sunlight in the way he thought it should be absorbed.

At the same time, this prosperous and rather self-indulgent man took to flirting with the ideas of Socialism. He got so far into the ideology that he invited Keir Hardie to stay with him at Shallott for a week-end, and the invitation was accepted. On the Saturday evening the butler, putting the final touches to the table, was professionally appalled to discover the guest in the lounge and *not dressed for dinner*. In fact, the miner's son from Lanarkshire wore carpet slippers and neither collar nor tie. It was for the butler a harrowing problem, and he did his best to suggest that the Labour leader should change into something more *comme il faut*, offering to produce spare garments from his master's wardrobe. But no; the fiery man of the I.L.P. supped in these easy clothes in his own home, and so he would dine in Shallott or not at all. There is no record of the experiment ever having been repeated.

We shall hear more of Adam later on. Meanwhile, jumping a generation ahead, we find another slightly eccentric bachelor Birkmyre in Kilmacolm. This was James, eighth child and third son of Henry II and therefore Adam's nephew. It will be seen later on that this man contributed valuably to the success of the family firm by concentrating on chemical methods of proofing cloth. His leisure hours were wholly given over to the enjoyment of horses. He set up a riding school in Kilmacolm; on fine days he rode downhill to Port Glasgow on one of his favourite mounts, 'Kitchener', a groom following on the spare horse.

He rode in point-to-point races all over the country and often enough cracked his ribs or a limb; the records of the Lanark and Renfrew Hunt reveal him as winner of point-to-point races on 'Flying Fox', 'Silver Crest' and 'Daily'. For a period he was Master of a Hunt in Yorkshire, catching a train every Friday evening during the season to lead the field at the Saturday morning meet.

One family legend is usually attached to James. It appears that, choosing to travel to Port Glasgow by carriage one day, he had to wait fully ten minutes for his coachman to turn up. The man was naturally scolded for the delay and had his employer's gold watch dangled before his embarrassed face. We cannot guess now at the severity of the reprimand or at the nature of the man's excuses. It is simply on record that, when the carriage returned James Birkmyre to his Kilmacolm house in the evening, he handed the coachman a gold watch the spit of his own and warned him kindly to keep his eye on it.

It was within the third generation that the Birkmyres took to looking for country places. The legend is that Henry II was the first to think of a small estate in the Highlands where he could get a little shooting, and it is told that his first exploration was to look at an estate in the Western Isles, probably Jura. He took one of his daughters with him on this trip, and during the week-end the girl was afflicted with a raging toothache. There was no dentist within many miles; in any event, the God-fearing natives would not stir a foot to provide transport. The experience of an island week-end with a beloved child in agony convinced Henry Birkmyre that he should cleave to the mainland, and in due course he acquired the estate of Carse at the mouth of West Loch Tarbert in the lovely South Knapdale district of Argyll. To this area the Birkmyre clan, generation by generation, has been faithful.

None of the properties they acquired included wide-ranging moors requiring the services of a platoon of gamekeepers. A place for the children in the summer, a little shooting and fishing—modest indulgences that taxation at modern levels makes nearly impossible. The Birkmyres never deserted their base at Port Glasgow to become lairds. Their attention to business was strict and consistent; the mill girls could depend on them.

'Ghosted' view of Port Glasgow Works from the air.

Chapter VI

THE GOUROCK AT HOME

When the partners of The Gourock Ropework Company bought Richardson's sugar refinery at Newark in 1868 they were extending their main manufacturing centre from one end of their long ropewalk to the other, from west to east. The minutes of those early days record decisions rather than the reasons for them, but a phrase in one suggests

75

that the move was made in order, first, to extend into a large building the growing number of processes and, second, to provide for easier handling of growing needs in the way of raw material.

The original mills, as we have seen, were on a hilly site near the present Port Glasgow railway station. The roads were quite singularly steep, and cartage must have been expensive. The new railway ran on a low level under the escarpment, and sidings could be provided on or near the new site. The refinery—always a 'sugar-house' in the local idiom—stood on the main road only a few feet above sea level, so that goods coming in by ship, whether through Greenock, Port Glasgow or Glasgow proper, were all the more easily brought to the doors of warehouses. Finally, a sugar refinery in those days was a tall building of

Rather a historic picture this. In the background the 'Brick Building', in the foreground the first lorry load of rope on its way to Leith for shipment to Russia. This was the first consignment in a barter deal which not only re-established The Gourock's old trading pattern of nearly 200 years before but, in 1958, was one of the first commercial breaks in the economic iron curtain between this country and Russia.

several floors, capable of being easily adapted to the complex processes of spinning, weaving and twisting.

The Gourock's building at the eastern end of Port Glasgow is indeed a landmark, all the more so when a great neon sign comes up in hours of darkness to proclaim its identity to all coming into the town by road or rail from the east—even to travellers by plane in and out of Renfrew Airport or by ship up river. It is doubtful, however, if even the most devoted investigator could exactly determine what is left of the building purchased from Messrs Richardson. In the course of nearly 100 years there have been fires, additions, adaptations, demolitions, reconstructions; most of these changes dictated by developments in manufacturing methods, so many of them latterly imposed by mechanisation. It is thus a vast, rambling mass of a place, so odd in its structure that a basement passage leading from one department to another runs under a street, another under the railway line to Gourock. It is a domestic joke that it takes a new man at least a week to learn his way about—and even then, he might be well advised to carry a map and compass!

Even so, any connoisseur of industrial history finds in these Port Glasgow works, so advanced in techniques, the most charming signs of ancientry. The textile trades are basic—one had almost said primitive—in their nature. As soon as man had discovered that certain natural products of the world about him could be so handled as to provide coverings and fastenings for himself and his goods, he devised a series of manufacturing processes that have remained constant throughout the ages, even if machinery has intervened to speed up the processes of production.

You start with vegetable material of a fibrous nature. You clean it and tease it out into a condition fit for spinning. You thus make yarn that can be woven into cloth or, in the special case of ropes, twisted in the diameters required. Between the extremes—between, say, binder twine and the exquisite ropes for a racing yacht; between a newsagent's delivery bag and a set of hatch covers for an ocean-going cargo vessel—the range is wide: all the more so since such synthetic fibres as nylon, Terylene, polythene and even more recent alternatives go into the finished article. One needs only to look at the deck of a modern fishing vessel in harbour to see how much delicacy and colour, along with great strength, has been added to her equipment within recent times.

77

Three of the above pictures show stages in processing of traditional fibres—sisal (top left), manila (top right) and flax (above). The fourth shows one stage in the processing of man-made fibres, in this case nylon. Important as the man-made fibres are in certain fields, it seems unlikely that they will completely oust the vegetable fibres in many of their traditional applications.

The synthetic fibres apart, The Gourock Ropework Company's mills at Port Glasgow deal largely with four vegetable fibres—manila from the Phillipines, flax from Europe and Russia, sisal from East Africa and soft hemp (that is, true hemp) from Europe and India. (It will be seen later on that the Company's New Lanark Mills are mainly concerned with cotton, largely from the Southern States of America, and with synthetics.) One may reflect that the Company's imports make a substantial contribution to the country's shipping business.

Manila, sisal and soft hemp, depending upon how they are processed and how finely they are prepared and spun, can provide ropes of widely differing characteristics and appearance, from the silky but very tough Italian hemp ropes of a racing yacht to the massive and

78

much less glamorous-looking sisal hauling-lines of an ocean tanker. But this can be misleading: even sisal, harder and coarser fibre though it may be, can also be made to produce a fine, smooth and pliable yacht rope, just as the silkier and tougher manila can be made up into an unwieldy-looking ship's towing spring of perhaps a massive 22 inches in circumference.

Flax, the fourth of these vegetable fibres, used to be made into rope at one time but nowadays its principal rôle is in the manufacture of canvas. As with cotton, it is woven into a range of canvases of different weights and constructions depending upon the use to which it is to be put. All of these, duly proofed by the 'dry' chemical proofing process first developed in this country by James Birkmyre and still bearing the family name, go literally all over the world in vast quantities as one of the Company's best-known and most enduring—and durable—products, Birkmyre's Cloth.

There is a rather paradoxical comment on record from an early Branch Manager of The Gourock's U.K. organisation concerning the unquestionable quality of the Company's products in the late days of sail: An East Indiaman rigged with Gourock hemp ropes and flax sails, held on with a heavy press of sail in an Indian Ocean storm. The sails held, the ropes held. As a result, the ship was lost—lost to the god of those days, the god of speed.

With the importation of flax from Russia history rhythmically repeats itself. The reader will recall from an earlier chapter the anxieties of Mr John Stevenson over his supplies from that area during the 18th century. We know that, during the 19th century, ships arrived regularly in the harbour of Port Glasgow, bringing in the raw materials— some of these ships owned by The Gourock. A few old men remember that one arrived each year with a full cargo of Archangel tar, the barrels carted to a large store within the mill at Newark, always known as 'the Tar Cellar'. The interchange has been resumed despite many political interventions, this time in the form of a sizeable barter-deal of Gourock ropes for Russian flax. This was a private barter arrangement, perhaps not cordially received by Whitehall in the first place, but the Russians are glad to exchange their raw materials for finished Gourock goods and the bargain has well satisfied both sides.

The processes are basic, simple but for the ingenuity of the machines that nowadays carry them out. Any attempt to describe

79

Equipped with the latest in heavy-duty high output Gill Spinners, with specially designed handling systems and with a complete conveyor delivery system, the 'Yankee Flat' at Port Glasgow is one of the most modern and most productive hard-fibre spinning and preparing plants in the world.

Operating at a speed which makes the older methods of beaming look as though they have come to a stop this high speed auto-beaming unit has hydraulic brakes and a tell-tale system that pin-points any one single faulty yarn out of the hundreds being beamed at any given time.

mechanical processes in words is, however, rather a waste of time. The thing has to be seen in action, especially on the grandiose scale of the operations in Port Glasgow. Looking down from one of its galleries on the vast expanse of what is called the Yankee Flat, the layman has the impression only of innumerable long machines turning and winding and clacking not a little in what seems to be a frenzy that only orchestral music, rather than words, could express. The scene has its majesty. But music could hardly be heard in that great cavern of mechanical noises, and the innocent's voice is strained, his ears drumming, when he asks why it should be called the Yankee Flat? As to that, more than one legend prevails. It is either because it was once equipped with machinery of American manufacture or because it once produced goods demanded by the American market.

Yet all this mass of cunning machinery is, essentially, going through the same motions as those of a Hebridean crofter making up his yarn for a length of tweed—or, for that matter, a Nubian peasant woman making up cotton yarn for her husband's white robe. The bales of raw materials are ripped open. The fibrous stuff within is batched, spread, combed and so formed into continuous ribbons of sliver. These are combined and combed, the operation repeated again and again until each individual fibre lies parallel with the others. Then at length they can be spun into a yarn of remarkable tensile strength, ready for the ropemaker. In the same way flax is hackled or carded in fine slivers and then combined and drawn, combined and drawn, until it is ready for spinning into cloth yarn. It is surprising how much of the work of preparing a rope or a length of cloth is taken up by those preliminary needs to tame the raw materials.

A School of Weaving, with looms in charge of an expert, deals with the new intake of female labour. The element of skill prevails. It does not nowadays require a battery of girls to watch the machines. Fifty years ago The Gourock employed the best part of 2,000 people at Port Glasgow; the labour force today numbers rather more than 700. But watch a specially skilled woman at work, spinning flax yarn from sliver or rove for the warp or weft yarns that go on to the weaver.

She is a calm woman in her thirties. Her hands on the whirling bobbins are firm, assured; she works so fast that she is always motioning her young assistants to fetch more and more. If and when a thread breaks, she stops the whizzing spool and mends the thread with a knot,

This streamlined package boiling plant—the first of its kind and size to be installed in Britain—has superseded nine separate operations which formerly had to be carried out in the treatment of flax cloth yarn before weaving.

After treatment in the package boiling plant flax cloth yarns are wound into hard 'cheeses' on these high-speed modern machines, ready for the final processes of warping and beaming before weaving into cloth.

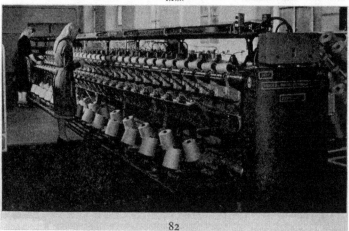

all in a flash that seems a single act of legerdemain. She is on piecework, to be sure, but she earns a weekly pay-packet a white-collared clerk might envy.

It may be observed in the meantime that flax requires more elaborate handling than any of the other materials used in the various processes. That is: between spinning and weaving it may for certain purposes have to be soaked in boiling water and then, in another deep vat, fortified by chemical treatment. The conical spools seem to be of a blueish-grey at this stage, but when the fabric comes off the looms it is seen to be cream-coloured, with a fine distinguishing selvedge line woven into it. It is thick and strong but pliable. Calendered, it takes on a handsome sheen, a material fit to be chemically treated and then

Specially woven for the purpose, the flax canvas of water bags or 'charguls' is so made as to allow a controlled rate of evaporation of the water from the surface of the water bag. This results in the water being kept relatively cool and fresh in even the hottest conditions. The water bag shown here is in service in Australia.

83

ready for years of wind and weather, years of wear and tear, whether on the deck of a ship or over the loads of long-distance lorries.

Flax is also made up into a beautiful fabric with the charming trade name of 'water bag canvas'. Fairly light in weight, and of striking whiteness, this material is mainly used for making up into containers in which water may be at once stored and cooled by 'breathing', especially in the hot regions of Australia.

A mere list of the special products of the Port Glasgow mills would fill a page of this book and more. In the meantime, it is sufficient to concentrate on the fact that Port Glasgow—as distinct from the branch establishments that will be accounted for later on—is arranged in its complexity to produce ropes, cordage and twines along with stout protective cloths, and these from four basic vegetable raw materials—manila, flax, sisal and hemp—along with, of course, the synthetic fibres. In fact, The Gourock's output of rope, cordage and twine tends to exceed in value that of any other of its products, and one can fancy that this would please old Henry Birkmyre I in the shades, for he developed from weaver to ropemaker first and foremost.

The art and science of ropemaking are very old, rooted in the earliest history of mankind; and to that fascinating subject this narrative will return in due course. For the time being it is well to pause for a little to consider the human aspects of life and work within such a large organisation as The Gourock and within the given setting under the Renfrewshire hills: in the small burgh that was to be the City of Glasgow's wonderful foreport.

It has already been seen that, amid the vast agglomeration of buildings that make up The Gourock mill as it is today there stands between the office block and storage premises two dwelling houses of some antiquity: one of three, the other of two storeys, probably built in the late 18th or early 19th century in the honest burghal style of Scotland. They are obviously the sort of houses in which the masters of a family business lived near their works, and at least one of these dwellings was in fact occupied by a Birkmyre partner until as recently as 1898—that is, more than 100 years after Henry I came to Port Glasgow as foreman. It gratifies the sense of history to know that the last Birkmyre born within those stone walls was destined to urge upon his fellow-directors the creation of a novel and valuable asset—the creation of a works laboratory.

84

Henry III.

This man was Henry Birkmyre III, son of John Birkmyre II and therefore grand-nephew of old John Birkmyre of Broadstone. He was a person of sensitive personality, and he died untimely; but the laboratory is in a way his memorial. It stands high on the hill behind the mill proper: so high that its windows look down on the roofs of the loftiest mill building and across the Clyde to the hills about Loch Lomond. It also looks into a large tank which serves the processes going on below, and from which, since it is refreshed from a moorland dam, more than one keen angler among the workers has taken a fat trout. One of the old hands, reminiscing, recalled how those steep slopes were in his day often covered by fabrics, presumably bleaching.

A further word must be said here about Henry III. At this period a very heavy load was laid upon his shoulders. To him fell the heavy task of running the works almost entirely and although in this he had the able assistance of John Cormie and John Kerr (later to become Sales Director), the combined load of work and war service took its toll and he died a relatively young man.

Looking north-west from the roof of the 'Brick Building' across the Clyde to the Gareloch and the hills of Dunbartonshire and Argyll.

He was largely instrumental in bringing the Ropemakers' Federation into being. The Gourock were trusted as a Company, Henry III as a man, and this greatly assisted in drawing towards association the various rather mutually suspicious entities within the British Cordage industry.

Those high roofs of what was always called the Brick Building were for a time given over to another sport. When young, the sons of William I took a fancy for breeding fighting cocks and, no doubt with the connivance of sporting parties among the workers, mains were held on the roof, far above the observation of legal authority. Information leaked to the police, however, and when the lads were one day watching their favourites in combat, word came up from the gatehouse to say that officers of the law had arrived to carry out a raid. The apparatus of cock-fighting was quickly cleared away, and the young Birkmyres scuttled quickly through one exit, locking the door behind them. In due course, suitably delayed, the police were shown up to the deserted roof, and then the youngsters, using their knowledge of the intricacies of the building, ran up and locked the only alternative entrance or exit. The pleasant legend—more likely, fact—is that the police officers were allowed to cool their heels up there for three hours on end.

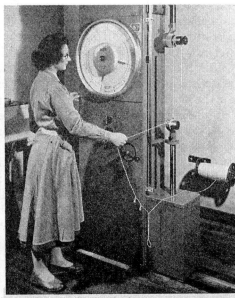

Above left: Routine colorimetric chemical analysis in progress using a Spekker photo-electric comparator.
Above right: On machines such as this, hundreds of physical strength tests are carried out daily on materials in progress and on finished products.

Above left: This Uster electronic yarn regularity tester—seen in use on flax tow sliver—ensures a high degree of control in uniformity of finished cloth yarns.

Above right: A micro-biologist examines mildew spores flown over specially from Central Africa after they have been bred in special cultures. Methods of preserving Birkmyre's Cloth from the attack of such mildews is part of the continuous battle waged in maintaining the rot-resisting qualities of Gourock products all over the world.

87

The laboratory, though expertly staffed, is not only a research establishment. Its functions are to see to the maintenance of standards of manufactured materials and to the development of existing lines. The routine testing of tensile strengths, the stabilisation of proper weights, the checking of durability in dyes and other colouring materials are essential parts of its business. Its chiefs work in admirable detachment on what workers on lower levels call 'Mount Olympus', for the choice of materials to be tested in one way or another is not left to a departmental head proud of a specially good batch of stuff; it is picked at random out of the run of the mill by cool young women in white overalls.

This is an unresting form of work. If abstract research is not its business, the laboratory must be tireless in looking for new materials or new blends of materials and continually engaged in the perfection and improvement particularly of those chemical substances that give cloth its weather- and wear-resisting qualities. Birkmyre's Cloth gave its inventors in the 19th century plenty of trouble. One old hand, Robert Hopkins, recalled the early days of patent proofing and the difficulties that arose out of inexperience before a laboratory existed.

Under elaborate automatic control, the coating of the base cloth with P.V.C. paste is the first stage in the production of Birkmyre's PluViaC Cloth.

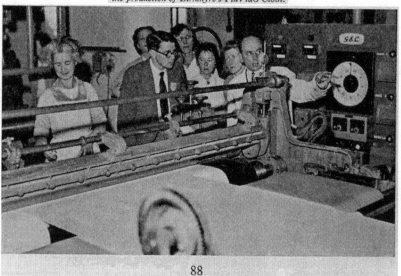

88

Marking of covers in the Paint Loft at Port Glasgow is one of the last stages in production before sending them literally all over the world.

The bolts of cloth had to be spread out full-length in the sail loft. If that were not done, the chemical mixtures generated so much heat that they would catch fire, and many bolts were destroyed in this way before James Birkmyre, Henry II's third son, worked out the proper formulae for the Birkmyre proprietary proofing which, as the first-ever 'dry' chemical proofing, has remained basically unchanged until today.

Robert Hopkins also remembered that the first large order for covers, 500 of them, came in 1889 from the Caledonian Steam Packet Co., for their fleet of river steamers run in conjunction with the Caledonian Railway Co., now working with the Scottish Region of British Railways under the British Transport Commission. These covers were woven from flax, each tarpaulin treated by being laid out flat and brushed with tar. Before a process of stencilling was perfected, the lettering was painted by hand on the material, and Hopkins saw James, Henry and Archie Birkmyre of the fourth generation industriously painting through the night to get the order delivered in time.

The proofing of canvas for covers is nowadays a highly mechanised business, but perhaps on that account requiring all the closer liaison between the laboratory and the departmental managers. The proofing flats at Port Glasgow are, so to speak, outside laboratories. Whatever the basic material of the cloth to be treated, all sorts must go through ingeniously constructed baths of chemicals, be dried off, hoisted to another floor and calendered, or put through a vast machine, longer and much taller than an express railway engine, to have special fire-resistant proofing applied.

Still newer proofings have been developed, P.V.C. coating of cloths for example. In this The Gourock has once more been one of the pioneers of the textile trade. Here, cloths of flax, cotton, nylon or Terylene are coated on one or both sides with a layer of specially plasticised poly-vinyl-chloride.

This coated material is then drawn to its last refinement through a sort of magic box of tricks, in which it is pressed again in a temperature of nearly 400°F., and when it comes out at length to the point where the men are waiting to gather it, the coated fabric—produced in a range of brilliant colours—is now tamed and folds itself meekly. Most of this material goes through under the registered trade name of PluViaC, and even the layman sees that it is a lovely job: the strong cloth as the foundation, the bright, shining coat of chemical substance symbolising the marriage of specialist chemistry and textile expertise. Old Henry Birkmyre I would not have been able to believe his sharp eyes.

The cloth finished, some of it becomes the raw material for tailoring on the grand scale. This portion goes to the lofty flats of the sail loft to be cut and sewn according to the customer's requirements. These flats of the mill are curiously silent after the hum and clatter and clack of the spinning and weaving departments. They are mostly empty of machinery, save one that seems a small forest of outsize sewing machines. Not far from the girls who supervise these engines, men and boys, controlling a battery of silent and almost automatic electronic machines, seal the long seams with strips of plastic material at heat and under high pressure—but with a strange absence of fuss.

Another flat is like a huge ballroom, the immediate foreground perhaps occupied only by one lone sailmaker squatting as he concentrates on some special task, while behind the screen against which he works a squad of young girls with an expertise born of considerable practice, deftly apply the customer's business style to the finished cover of blue, green, red, yellow or whatever colour he has chosen for his own display purposes. In a quiet bay of one flat a middle-aged woman kneels with heavy needle and twine on a cover that, a casualty of commercial war after years of use, has been sent back to The Gourock to be patched and reproofed, as a man will send a favourite suit to be cleaned and, occasionally, mended.

So to the ground floor again and the towering hills of material in store—binder twine, cordage in a wide range of materials and diameters, heavy ropes, hawsers.

The world is being supplied from these caverns, and the range of specific products put out · from Port Glasgow, over and above contracted orders, is staggering in length and variety.

Obviously, all the late advances in the new fields of manufacture would have been impossible without the work done in the laboratory up on the hillside, so vastly expanded since it was set up in 1936. Testing, improving, experimenting, especially with the fine fabrics and brilliant dyes of today are unresting tasks in our competitive age. It has been explained that this laboratory is not a research establishment proper, but in 1948 the Directors of The Gourock Ropework Company declared their faith and continuing interest in the development of their trades by the establishment in the University of Glasgow of a bursary worth £250 a year to any scientist willing to undertake organised research into the qualities of hard fibres.

One wonders what Baldie Cameron, rope-spinner and bellringer in Gourock, would have made of it all.

Robert Owen

Chapter VII

THE GOVERNMENT OF NEW LANARK

When The Gourock Ropework Company absorbed the Lanark Spinning Company in 1903 it took into its fold a manufacturing unit which, though considerably younger than itself, had attracted much more public, even international, attention. The mills at New Lanark were the laboratories in which Robert Owen had conducted his remarkable social experiments during the early decades of the 19th century.

On the centenary of Owen's death, which took place in 1858, more than one excellent book was issued in commemoration of a man who, perhaps before his time, was an astonishingly bold and successful pioneer of so many aspects of industrial life taken for granted today—welfare, work study, the co-operative system of shopping, infant welfare and so on. Some of these works, however, tended to ignore the fact that the great Welshman owed much to the Scotsman who became his father-in-law, David Dale, himself a pioneer of good industrial relations, though not on the highly organised scale that in the end turned Owen into something of a crank with his 'Government of New Lanark'.

Dale was born the son of a small shopkeeper at Stewarton, Ayrshire, in 1739. In the traditional way of country boys in Scotland he started earning, probably a pittance and his keep, as the herd of a neighbouring farmer's cattle. Thence he went on to serve part of his apprenticeship as a weaver in Paisley and finished it in other establishments about Glasgow. A journeyman, he took to the road with a pack, and he made it his business to buy the woven fabrics—mainly linen at first—sold by peasant women at cottage doors. Soon enough he was set up in Glasgow as a merchant, and he was among the first in Britain to import textile goods from the Low Countries. He became a banker, and he became very rich at an early age. At the same time, he perceived that cotton fabrics would ultimately replace the traditional Scottish linen, and he followed with interest the developments of mechanised spinning and weaving then taking place in the North of England, being specially impressed by Arkwright's water-driven machine.

Arkwright visited Glasgow in 1783 and was soon in touch with Dale. The latter became enthusiastic over the former's water frame; within a day or two he had the inventor out to look at the Falls of Clyde near Lanark. They decided right away to build a mill on a site nearest the point at which the great head of water in the falls could most advantageously be used to power the looms. To this joint venture Dale contributed his capital, Arkwright his rights in the use of the machines. The first mill was working in 1785, employing some 250 persons.

It was the inventor who had visualised New Lanark as 'the Manchester of Scotland'—a fate it has happily escaped—but the partnership was soon broken, and abruptly. The legend runs that Dale had caused a bell under a wooden belfry to be set up at one end of the first mill, and that Arkwright, seeing it for the first time, observed tartly that it was a damned silly place to put a bell. Dale is said to have defended

Lying in a bend of the upper Clyde Valley just below the Dundaff Lynn Falls the village and mills of New Lanark have remained outwardly almost unchanged over the years. Inwardly, these mills now house one of the most productive and modern plant-systems in the country. Almost in time with the small church, centre of the photograph, is 'Rosedale' the house at one time occupied by David Dale, Robert Owen's father-in-law.

himself with spirit, and the tale goes that the partners, repairing to an inn in the old town of Lanark proper, decided to dissolve the partnership. It is an engaging legend, but one may doubt if two successful men, each with the matter of greatness in him, would have split on such a trivial issue. Perhaps the affair of the bell merely symbolised a profound psychological rift between them; each was a man of means who could afford to go his own way.

That fatal bell has its own story. It was cast in Glasgow in 1786 and intended, as an inscription round the flange suggests, for 'Hagars Town, Washington County, Lutheran Congregation'. Why it was never shipped to that destination remains a mystery.

Dale had in the meantime started to build a second mill, and in that he was lucky. It was nearly completed when the first mill went up in flames in 1788, throwing more than 200 people out of work. David Dale was remarkable in admitting that he had made a great deal of money, and proud of having made it, but it was also his justifiable boast that he was always willing to put it back into circulation for the benefit of the workers. In his day he set up mills in various parts of Scotland, some of them with the specific aim of checking the depopulation of the Highlands. David Livingstone was employed as a child in a mill he set up at Blantyre, also in Lanarkshire. As for the results of the fire at New Lanark, Dale kept his displaced workers in employment on salvage work and on preparations for rebuilding. This cost him more than £2,000 in wages.

A glance at the map shows that New Lanark is still removed from large centres of population, and David Dale's chief trouble was to assure himself of a supply of labour. It is told that when, in 1791, a ship filled with emigrants from the West Highlands bound for North America put back into Greenock under stress of weather, he hurried down to that port and enlisted 200 hands for his mills. He built houses, virtually creating the village of New Lanark. Finally, he followed a custom of the period and appealed to local authorities in Glasgow and Edinburgh to provide him with pauper children, and from these sources he acquired large supplies of cheap labour.

It seems incredible now, but these infants, taken into the mills at between five and eight years of age, apprenticed for periods of anything from seven to ten years, worked from 6 a.m. until 7 p.m., with one half hour for breakfast and one hour for dinner—11½ hours each day.

The belfry shown in this general view of part of the village street at New Lanark houses the famous bell, the siting of which led to the split in partnership between Dale and Arkwright. The picture on the right (with the Saltire Society's plaque above the door) shows how the bell is rung morning and lunch-time every day to this day. (This is merely to observe an old tradition as all other stopping and starting times in the works are electrically signalled.)

Then Dale, his intentions all for the best, had them attend school until 9 p.m., organising classes for religious instruction on Sundays.

It is necessary, however difficult it may be, to realise that his system of managing child labour was in its day regarded as enlightened. All we can now say is that he obviously meant better than most of his contemporaries. It is on record that, during one long period of shortage, he imported cargoes of food and sold them at cost price to his people. But we cannot wonder that the Radical feelings were always strong among the spinners. Even during Dale's lifetime it became obvious that a child, heavy in brain and eye after an interminably long day's work, could not profit in the least from a session of teaching in the evening.

David Dale's was nevertheless an experiment in labour management far ahead of the then current practice, and at New Lanark it was duly extended by Robert Owen to form an exercise in effective Socialism, an attempt to create a viable Utopia, so remarkable as to attract world-wide attention and visitors from distant countries: the latter including a Grand Duke of Russia, Nicholas, who profited so little from his visit that he became one of the most despotic of Tsars.

As suggested, the achievements of Robert Owen can be more profitably studied in the many volumes written about him and his career. The fifth son of an ironmonger-saddler, he was born at Newtown, Montgomeryshire, in 1771. He entered the textile business through experience of the drapery trade in various parts of England, and he was well employed in Manchester, in a wholesale and retail establishment, while still in his teens. At the age of only eighteen, affected by the stirrings of invention about him, he became partner in a firm manufacturing the new machinery for cotton spinning. This arrangement breaking down through the sloth of his partner, Owen went into the spinning business with the Chorlton Twist Company, prospering tolerably well. He was ultimately offered a partnership in the considerable firm of Borrowdale & Atkinson, charged with both the management of the

These are typical entries from Owen's personal diary which he obviously carried with him as he went around the mills and in which he made notes of all points of interest to him—any shortage of water causing a drop in the speed of machines; any faulty products he noticed; points for action regarding the behaviour of employees, and so on.

mills and the selling of the fine yarns they produced. It was as a traveller for his firm's goods that he first came to Glasgow.

It is said that Owen there met David Dale's daughter and eldest child, and that it was the young lady who suggested that he should look at New Lanark. However that may be, the establishment on the Falls of Clyde seemed to the young Welshman to be the ideal site for the industrial and social experiments that had long occupied his thoughts. Returning to Manchester, he got the promise of solid financial support and in due course returned to Glasgow with two firm propositions to make. He took over Dale's interest in New Lanark and married the daughter. His reign at New Lanark began on a date easily remembered—January 1st, 1800.

This Robert Owen was by any standard of measurement a man far out of the ordinary and, in his thinking, far in advance of his time. Whatever one may think privately of the effects of Socialism in State practice, he made a magnificently honest effort to put the general theory into effect within the manageable proportions of an isolated unit—and perhaps that was the flaw inherent in his reasoning. His more learned biographers suggest that he passed from the general idea of co-operation to practical Socialism; we may see him as a practical Communist before Karl Marx was born. We may even suspect that he fell ultimately into the temptations of dictatorship.

Duly established as king of the castle in his remote bailiwick, Owen started at once to tackle the abuses associated with the lavish use of child labour. The New Lanark community then consisted of about 1,300 people, with up to 500 children brought in for work from the surrounding parishes. The new manager's first decision was to stop the recruitment of pauper labour, to reduce the number of hours a child should work, and to raise the age at which an infant should be allowed to start work in the mills. In the first place, however, he had to tackle some bad habits that had grown up within the community— pilfering in the works, drunkenness, slovenliness in the homes. He even went the length of setting up behind each worker's place, for everybody to read, a sort of coloured indicator called A Silent Monitor that indicated the management's assessment of the worker's progress or decline in industrial and social efficiency.

This measure did not make for popularity, but the excellence of his intentions did declare itself slowly. He discovered that the

'The Government Inspector', perhaps a rather sinister figure by today's standards. The 'kindly' Government Inspector checks that the little girls employed in a cotton mill are not working more than twelve or fifteen hours a day.

workpeople were being grossly overcharged in the small local shops, and he set up one of his own on co-operative lines. The shop is there to this day. He built more and better houses, public halls and places of worship. He established a register of births, deaths and marriages. Owen finally won the confidence and support of his workpeople in 1806. In that year the U.S. Government placed an embargo on the export of cotton to Great Britain, and the consequences were disastrous throughout the textile regions of this country. Owen firmly decided, however, that those he regarded as his charges should not suffer. Throughout the four months of the embargo period he kept his workers busy on the maintenance of the New Lanark mills at a cost of £7,000 in wages.

The man's idealism had him in trouble more than once during his middle years, and it wrecked him in the long run. His first partners in the venture were hard Lancashire businessmen, not at all inclined towards social experiment, and they came down on him for what they regarded as his excessive expenditure on *amenities*. A second group of financiers abandoned him. But Robert Owen was by this time a man of consequence in Britain. He had taken to writing and lecturing on his pet theories and had won the admiration of the country's benevolent intellectuals, the influence of the French Revolution still working strongly. He therefore went to London and had little difficulty in raising sufficient money to buy out the second group of partners. Jeremy Bentham and a group of rich Quakers were among his backers.

So the good work proceeded. Owen had now laid it down that dividends were to be restricted to 5 per cent, an absurdly low rate of interest in the then prosperous state of the textile industry. At the same time his projects multiplied, and he came to the point of planning settlements in various parts of the world that would reproduce the self-contained, co-operative features of his 'Government of New Lanark'. In the second half of the 20th century we may be allowed to see an element of comedy in the proceedings that led up to what was for Owen tragic failure.

His leading principle, and a sound one, was that the improvement of society in general could only come through educational advances. To that end he built schools, their costs and maintenance coming out of profits; he opened at New Lanark the 'Institute for the Formation

Robert Owen's School for the Formation of Character (from the original drawing by Danek).

of Character' in 1816. One room was set aside for infants up to four years of age, and they were simply to play—indoors in inclement weather, outdoors as often as possible. This room was really the first infant school to be set up in Britain, and it was quite astonishingly advanced in being furnished with large coloured maps and pictures, mainly of objects of natural history; the conventional paraphernalia of pedagogy in 1960. The children were never to hear a voice raised in anger.

The long-term plan was that no child should start work in the mills before the age of ten, and Owen hoped to raise this leaving age to twelve in due course. Thus, between the infant school and the leaving age, the children passed through a regulated course of sound education, with sewing and knitting for the girls thrown in, military drill for the boys. Dancing and singing were encouraged; and an infant with a taste for music could choose an instrument and be taught how to play it.

And all this cost a lot of money. The day came when even the Quaker financiers in London began to wonder if the practical idealist at New Lanark was not going a bit too far. They sent representatives to Scotland, and the good Quakers, discovering that the boys of the community were encouraged to dance in kilts, laid it down that males over six years of age should wear trousers or drawers! But there was no containing Owen's enthusiasms. Spreading his notions throughout Great Britain, he advocated co-operative shops, labour exchanges, a back-to-the-land policy that adumbrated the setting-up of 'Villages of Co-operation'; he framed a Factory Act; he formed the 'Grand National Trades Union'. He was, in short, a Communist before his time, and he suffered for that.

Inevitably, Owen's notions, so many now accepted as commonplace, incensed most of the industrialists of his period. His main error in tactics appears to have been the delivery—in London, in 1817—of an address in which he appeared to attack formal religion, though he was more likely getting at those who, making a parade of piety, were profiting by exploitation of cheap labour in admittedly shocking conditions. In the long run, but not before he had made a heavy impact on British thinking about industrial conditions, Owen withdrew from New Lanark in 1827; and how he fared thereafter, an innovator to the end of his 77 years of life, the reader will find in any good study of his career.

One or two aspects of the Dale–Owen saga seem of curious interest. Both men of outstanding gifts, so closely related by business ties and marriage, both turned in old age towards the more unconventional forms of religious belief. Originally a member of the Church of Scotland, David Dale ultimately founded a sect, or congregation, of his own, the 'Old Scots Independents', and appointed himself its pastor. It is now among the many half-forgotten curiosities of Scottish ecclesiastical history. In his declining years Robert Owen sought solace in Spiritualism.

Three souvenirs of Robert Owen's reign at New Lanark are valued possessions of The Gourock Ropework Company today, one a good portrait in the Board Room and another is a 'Ticket for Wages' to the value of five shillings, in form something like a banknote. In those days of low wages it was common for large employers, especially in the textile trades, to issue tokens for services rendered, these to be exchanged for goods under the unhappy Truck system. In most cases the tokens were old Spanish dollars countermarked with their worth in British wages, and these coins have been extensively studied and

Payment of wages at New Lanark. The 'Ticket for Wages' above, printed and issued from New Lanark, is perhaps unique in character. It was cashable only at the New Lanark General Store. The same applied to the countermarked silver dollar (below), again overstamped at New Lanark, this being a method of payment probably originally introduced into Scotland by David Dale.

catalogued by numismatists. It is probable that coins were used at New Lanark before Owen's time—Dale appears to have used them at an earlier period—but it better suited Owen's orderly mind to issue his well-printed vouchers, signed by himself and, presumably, his cashier. Experts are inclined to think that he was in breach of the law in issuing these paper tokens, since an Act of 1813 forbade the issue of promissory notes for amounts less than £1, but perhaps the 'Government of New Lanark' was above that sort of thing.

The third piece is a document that turned up in the New Lanark offices long after Owen's death. By all tests of handwriting, style and historical sequence it undoubtedly is his own production.

This is a small notebook in which a busy man jotted rough notes in careless handwriting; and one fancies that its main purpose was to refresh his memory when he should have to explain to his partners occasional lags in output. Thus there are many notes about ice on the waters of the Clyde, the lowering of water power and decreases of revolutions in the mill machinery. Along with figures of outstanding production, which mean little to us now but obviously gave him pleasure, he notes cases of slacking and thieving, naming the delinquents in each event. Current prices of raw material are mere incomprehensible jottings. But the disciplinarian, the near-dictator, comes up as when, on May 20th, 1820, he records: 'The village boys are requested to give up playing at the shinty or clubs and throwing stones, as they are by the first practice destroying the woods, and by the latter breaking windows and sometimes hurting persons.' The juveniles of New Lanark apparently counter-attacked according to their lights, for an entry two months later reports: 'The village boys cautioned against attacking the yeomen with foul language, etc.' Presumably the 'yeomen' belonged to some sort of internal police force Owen had set up.

This casual notebook is specially remarkable in suggesting that Owen anticipated Willett in the matter of Daylight Saving. He makes more than one reference to adjustments as between the works clock and the church bells. Specifically, on March 2nd, 1818, he notes: 'No light. Ten minutes taken off dinner hour for one week', and on March 23rd, 'The clocks kept ½ hour before Lanark.' For October 12th in the same year the entry runs 'Lighted up. Clocks put back half-an-hour,' but Owen relented on November 1st, noting: 'Rang the bell on Sabbath by Lanark clocks.'

One would fain linger over other features of this document, such as his concern for pregnant women among the workers—though he does not fail to observe the effect of this condition on output—and his distinction between married women and 'unfortunates'. But it is all an old story now, and Owen left New Lanark to lose most of his fortune in attempts to establish co-operative communities in various parts of the world. He was missed by his people; towards the end almost his only supporters in Scotland were his workers. The mills were taken over by a firm called Walker & Co., and old hands testified that those following Owen's departure were 'sore years'. Wages were reduced, the 'Truck' system of buying was made compulsory. The schools were neglected until an Act of Parliament introduced a School Board to take them over.

The acquisition of the New Lanark mills in 1881 was a private, extra-mural adventure by Henry Birkmyre II in conjunction with his brother-in-law, R. G. Sommerville. The latter was in the timber trade, still important to the economy of a shipbuilding centre before the industry turned wholly to iron and steel; he was a man of sufficient quality and local standing to become, like his brother-in-law, Provost of Port Glasgow. There is ample evidence to the effect that, specialising in the production of nets, they secured a good market for a good article.

One New Lanark veteran has told in an admirable summary of the history of the establishment how he was received in Holland when he went there as a young man prior to the opening of an agency in that country.

'I was told of fishermen coming in from outlying districts and asking particularly for "Lanrick" yarns, and our fishing nets were in appearance and quality second to none. "Lanrick" goods were well known, and among some of the customers the traveller who went round before the branch in Holland was opened was called "Mr Lanrick". When I went round with him at first I was called "Mr Lanrick's son", and on one occasion, after a misunderstanding with one of these customers, he said that he would tell my father about me, and that my father wouldn't have treated him like that.' (Lanrick is the traditional spelling and pronounciation of the place name.)

This witness also records that the whole management of the New Lanark establishment came under the hand of Henry Birkmyre II in

1888, though we imagine that his brothers were not without his confidence. It will be shown later on how the equipment and functions of the New Lanark mills were altered from time to time under the wider control of The Gourock Ropework Company, but the properties and goodwill of the Lanark Spinning Company were certainly valuable additions to the assets of the parent concern in Port Glasgow.

If Robert Owen could revisit New Lanark today he would not feel that it had greatly changed in its physical aspects. It is not the self-contained industrial unit it once was, for many of the 300-odd workers now come in from far and near by bus, while many of the tenement houses along the village streets are occupied by tenants who have nothing to do with the mills on the fringe of the Clyde below. Yet it remains itself compact, a place apart, with a curious air of the antique about it: such a tidy monument of good planning during the earliest years of the Industrial Revolution and of intelligent maintenance since then that only a few years ago, the Saltire Society, a body concerned with Scottish cultural affairs, awarded a plaque in recognition of The Gourock Ropework Company's thoughtful regard for the preservation of old amenities.

The character of New Lanark resides mainly in its apparent remoteness in a sort of cul-de-sac, quite a narrow gorge by the river. It can only be approached down a steep road that, about a mile south of Lanark proper, tumbles towards the Clyde past the gates of Braxfield House, now an empty shell. It was from the Braxfield estate that David Dale bought the lands for his first mills, and it was the McQueens of Braxfield who threw up that ogre of the Scottish judiciary, with the judicial title of Lord Braxfield, who was the 'original' of Robert Louis Stevenson's *Weir of Hermiston*.

So it is a square mile of territory historic in two departments. The group of mill buildings on the water's edge, fashioned out of a honey-coloured stone, has a look of charming antiquity. The lade still runs deep and strong from the mill-dam fed by the Clyde, and a cunning man may still lift a good fish out of it—as in the deep pool below the falls just above the buildings—but that strong stream can still drive a turbine powering one of the mills with some 650 b.h.p.

The importance of water in the earlier phases of the textile industry was never more lucidly illustrated than at New Lanark. To be sure, the bulk of the power now taken into the mill is in the form of electricity,

107

This is Caithness Row. To these houses, emigrants from Caithness, on their way to the New World and storm-stayed at the Tail of the Bank off Greenock, were brought by David Dale and there remained. On the left of the picture is the present General Store and Post Office which has been successively butcher's shop and baker's shop but, nevertheless, dates from Robert Owen's time.

but it is proper to remember that most of it is generated by water-power initially.

One mechanical feature of the New Lanark Mills is now legendary. This was a turbine of Swedish manufacture that, driven off the many waters about the place, supplied power before the public supply became available. This power was piped to the village, and there are many who remember how the lights could be seen burning in humble windows night and day, so negligible the cost of supplies. This excellent engine had to be stopped only once during its many years of service.

There have been changes in the group of mill buildings since Robert Owen reigned there. A few blocks consumed by fire have had to be replaced, but one or two of the originals still stand, allowing the observer to see how much better the Scots could build in stone than their sons did when they discovered the cheapness of red brick. Owen's

This peaceful scene is to be found right in the heart of the Mills of New Lanark. This part of the Mill Lade carries the overspill from the turbines which power the Mill.

'Institute for the Formation of Character' is still there behind its classical portico and today the ground floor makes a capacious works canteen. But the atmosphere remains.

It was on that upper floor that the dancing and drill classes were held. An elegant little musicians' gallery still stands against the southern wall, the fine ironwork intact, and visitors from far afield come to look at it, as if to worship at a shrine. They will tell you in New Lanark of one architectural student from the United States who came specifically to examine the newel posts of the iron stair leading to the gallery. He knew from his reading that they were of an unusual four-leaved clover design—and indeed they are!

Such as the American student could have seen that an ancient art plied at New Lanark was that of weaving baskets to holds cops and pirns of yarn. It was plied by Timothy O'Connell in his own corner under the Musicians' Gallery, and the accompanying photograph on the opposite page emphasises the beauty and interest of the setting.

Henry Birkmyre III used the New Lanark mill mainly for the production of nets. Taking over from the Walker family in 1881, he brought in net looms from Johnstone in Renfrewshire and expert workers to handle them and teach the local operatives the new arts. It had been intended by The Gourock Ropework Company that the works at Lynedoch Street, Greenock, would take over the business of net manufacture, but that move was delayed by an odd historical accident, as we shall see. In 1902 the New Lanark concern—by then virtually, if not legally, fused with the parent concern in Port Glasgow—took over some small net factories in Peel, Isle of Man, and executives were sent from Scotland to supervise them. It was eventually decided to transfer these looms to New Lanark, and for a time the payroll there bore such typical Manx names as Quayle and Caine, including, says one record with tantalising vagueness, 'a number of fishermen'.

Using willows steeped in the mill lade close by, old Timothy O'Connell plies his ancient trade making carrying baskets for process work in the mill.

The rather delicate Musicians' Gallery in the 'New House' built by Robert Owen not long after he had opened his School for the Formation of Character.

New Lanark is nowadays concerned mainly with the production of one of The Gourock's staples—canvas. It has come to deal to some extent with the new synthetic fabrics, nylon and Terylene in particular, and it will run you up a line in strong yarns for net-making, twines of various tensile strengths, and even fine material for the purposes of chemical filtration. In the main, however, the business of those old mills beside the Clyde is to produce cloth from cotton brought in mainly from the Southern States of America. All the processes are highly mechanised; many of the girls standing over the long frames are merely machine-minders. One feels, however, that Robert Owen, looking at the modern looms, would have understood and approved. He would most certainly approve the clean and well lit conditions in which they work, the comfortable homes they come from, the good food they get in the canteen; the good wages an attentive girl can earn. One may imagine that he could even conjure up a smile to realise that the delight of the younger girls is, in fact, dancing.

The production of cloth from cotton is a bit of a miracle in the layman's eyes. It is miraculous to see how the oblong bales of the raw

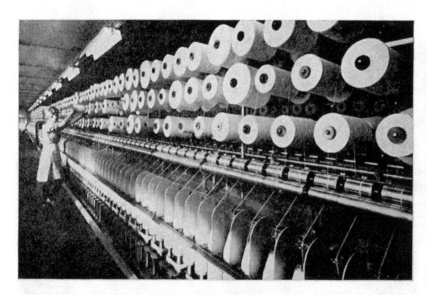

These two photographs embody the character of the now re-modelled New Lanark Mills. Over £250,000 has been spent on thoroughly modernising plant and flow-systems. It is interesting to note the original stone floors and arched roofs now housing ultra-modern machinery with its attendant fluorescent lighting, complicated heating, ventilating and humidifying systems.

stuff can so quickly be cleaned of their many impurities and then, through one machine after another, come out in streams of pure white, getting finer and finer until they are reduced to thin threads of surprising strength. This is the stuff that, beautifully wound, goes on to the looms to be woven into strong cloth, but it is under close observation all the way. One may well wonder at the skill of a matronly woman who examines each bundle of yarn as it comes along, in the shape of a small cheese, discerns any flaw in it at a glance, marks the spot of weakness with a small cross in red pencil, and throws it into a bin to be returned for reprocessing. The student of behaviour may note that many of these women choose to work in bare feet among the tufts of cotton that inevitably drift over the floors.

Yes: Robert Owen would have understood; and looking back from the mills towards the village he governed he would not discern many physical differences. There it is, cocked up on the steep eastern slope of the gorge, the village stretching along its short and only street. He would see in the foreground, among drying greens and vegetable gardens running down to the lade, the house used by David Dale,

This was New Lanark's contribution to the Lanimer Day Celebrations at the turn of the century. In the background can be seen the Birch Carriers who use their birch branches for beating the boundaries, a custom as old as the Lanimer Fair itself.

Rosedale, and the larger dwelling he used for himself. He would see that a small church in a Victorian architectural style has been built high behind the houses since his time, but he would see that the bell, said to have caused the rift between Dale and Arkwright, is under a small belfry on top of the central tenement building of the group and above the top flat in which he established the first church of all. It still rings twice a day for the purposes of the mills, and it rings on Sundays to call the people to worship in the little kirk behind.

Even as this history was in the final stages of preparation, it was announced that New Lanark was to renew its youth. This came of a decision by the directors of The Gourock Ropework Company to spend something like £250,000 on new machinery, involving a rearrangement of manufacturing spaces within the mills and considerable alterations, for the better, in the working conditions of the 300 employees.

Briefly, British-made machinery will introduce the 'sliver to spinning' system—that is one in which a single machine accepts the cleaned and carded fibre at one end, so to speak, and turns it out tightly spun at the other. The general effect will be to reduce the factory space now given over to the production of cotton goods, though not by any means to reduce the output, and leave more space available for larger, ever-expanding production of goods from the man-made fibres—nylon, polythene, Terylene and the rest. The water power so long drawn from the Clyde will be transformed into electricity to drive the new machines and heat the mills.

On the human side, the change will mean the introduction of a double day shift weaving system with women and an all-male night shift. The solid trade unionist is apt to equate modernisation with redundancy but that will not happen at New Lanark, so excellent are the prospects of expansion. Almost all the workers will have their weekly stints reduced from 42½ to 37½ hours without any loss of pay, and without reduction of piecework or bonus rates; and when they voted on the issue, their unions taking part, the majority in favour of the new scheme was large.

So here is a renewal of the vitality of a historic centre of production, and one feels that David Dale and Richard Arkwright would be gratified.

The Ropemaker's Certificate granted to Henry Birkmyre I in 1808.

Chapter VIII

ROPES AND MEN

In the Board Room of The Gourock Ropework Company at Port Glasgow there hangs, piously framed, an ornate document of much historical interest. This certifies that Henry Birkmyre I was admitted a member of the Gourock, Greenock and Port Glasgow Ropemakers' Society on July 29th, 1808. The Secretary who made out the testimonial was, we may hope, a better craftsman than he was a scribe, for he contrived to spell the recipient's Christian name as 'Hendry'.

The certificate is quite a charming pictorial piece of its period, delicately tinted. Its upper half is occupied by a fancy design, in which we see the wharves and ships of the lower Clyde ports precariously presided over by a god or goddess—the sex is hard to determine—who clings to an anchor on a monstrous lump of rock. The lower half, in two sections, illustrates more graphically the processes of ropemaking by hand . . . and they do not differ greatly from those displayed on the wall of a tomb of the 5th dynasty revealed at Thebes. No doubt the bulrushes that sheltered Moses provided the raw material in the latter case.

On the face of it, man probably had the Rope before he had the Wheel. There is no record of Noah using cables for the management of the Ark, but it is obvious that quinqueremes of Nineveh, Arab dhows of prehistoric design, Viking ships and the primitive catamaran of Southern seas needed cordage, even if only in the form of leather thongs. The Kon-Tiki voyage reproduced primeval conditions, and one may see almost any day at harvest time how a farmer's boy will almost instinctively twist or plait some sort of rope out of straw.

The interest of the Port Glasgow print is in its illustration of the method of ropemaking by hand. It depicts the worker, walking backwards, twisting the yarn under his strong fingers. Each man is shown as having a hank or 'head' of this hackled yarn round his waist, and once some fibres of this had been attached to a hook on a spinning wheel, he spun his yarn to the specification required. Slung to his belt was a pannikin of whale oil, with which he at once lubricated his hands and the fibre under his fingers.

The technicalities of the trade are innumerable and, to the layman, baffling; the point is that the manufacturer can advise the customer as to the best 'lay' for his purpose and then supply it in infinite varieties of weight, material, diameters and twists. We all see ropes in daily use and have a good working idea of their dimensions in relationship to their function; from the housewife's slender clothes line to the stouter cordage required to support, say, the strain of a staging used by painters high up on the face of a building. The specialist ropes and hawsers required for heavy duty purposes—for the mooring of a huge Atlantic liner or for towing a redundant battleship from Portsmouth to the Clyde—are of a gigantic order the layman almost never has the opportunity of seeing. In an admirable catalogue of its ropes, twines and cords issued by The Gourock Ropework Company to its customers, the writer of the historical section notes:

Typical of the huge towing springs produced at Port Glasgow this 4½-ton Admiralty Towing Spring in 22-inch circumference Manila gives a good idea of some of the domestic handling problems involved.

'In making hawsers and cables, stretching and laying were most laborious, needing the united strength of 70 to 80 men. By the end of the 18th century the limit of animal power seemed to have been reached. The size of ships increased, and it was said that the cables of a man-of-war were 18 inches to 24 inches in circumference and weighed from 4 to 7½ tons per 120 fathoms. The time had come for machinery.'

A Captain Joseph Huddart in the service of the East India Company was the most successful designer of the desirable mechanism, and though he failed to persuade established ropemakers to take up his invention, with the help of friends he got a factory built at Limehouse and had the satisfaction of seeing it in production early in the 1800's. Huddart's devices have naturally been greatly refined since his death in 1816 but, as we have noted, the mechanical process uncannily reproduces those illustrated in the certificate awarded to the first Henry Birkmyre.

The old plate illustrates the ropemaking processes by hand—the backward parade of the workers as they twist the strands by hand through oiled rags—then the physical battle of a number of men to twist the rope made up out of the strands. Huddart's principle was to pull the strands towards a drum, the strands passing through the orifices in a revolving 'register plate' to ensure absolutely regular laying of the finished article over the drum. Even so, the skill has never been taken out of the job. The ropelayer's eye is still keen as he follows the bogey, the 'top cart'; he is attended on his long parade down the ropewalk by a female acolyte who dutifully pulls open the wooden gates—the stakeheads—that separate the strands of the job in hand. Those gates are to this day exactly as shown in the print of 1808.

Over and above the certificate awarded to Henry Birkmyre I in 1808, the archives at Port Glasgow include a dissertation on the science of ropemaking, a domestic production. This is 'A Treatise on Rope-making' by Robert Freeland, Master Ropemaker to The Gourock Ropework Company, dated 1857, and respectfully presented by 'an Operative . . . with all respects' to his employers. Freeland's discourse is written in impeccable copperplate, but so small that a large magnifying glass and a lot of time are required to decipher it.

The treatise is concerned at length with technical details no lay reader could possibly follow, but it confesses an intense pride in the historical status of ropemaking and a confidence that, in these 1850's, it was still a staple industry within the economies of quite small seaports. And it is indeed well to remember that before the industry became so largely centralised and highly mechanised as it is today, there was at least one locally owned ropework near the smallest of British harbours, their former importance memorialised all round our British coasts in the names of streets and lanes.

It is well, too, to remember that the same Robert Freeland, as a retired master-ropemaker, must have begun his apprenticeship before 1800 and that he would then, almost certainly, be tutored by some older ropelayers who could well remember the very origins of the firm in 1736!

Highly mechanised today, ropemaking remains a fascinating and beautiful process, the feeling of tradition lingering. The speed with

Part of the most interesting schedule of ships and rigging which appears in Robert Freelund's 'Treatise on Ropemaking', further references to which are to be found on pages 173 and 174.

which the raw material is handled by the machines enhances, indeed, the fascination of the production of goods destined to be put to so many romantic uses. Sisal in the raw alone possesses aesthetic quality in its long, undulant strands and ivory colour. The processes of cleaning and hackling and spinning are straightforward, but when the yarn is at length wound on the bobbins, and this yarn is hauled on rapid machines to make the stouter strands; and when the strands are laid along the length of the ropewalk into a rope—then you have a concrete illustration of the poetry of motion. From beginning to end the process suggests the elegant motions of a fluid pouring along a smooth channel, and the idle layman may feel that here is a theme for the ballet. And a length of cordage duly coiled for the market is a tidy thing to see, the perfection of traditional workmanship; clean, strong, fit for the job.

It is an oddity of the ropemaking trade that in this country the girth of a fibre rope is usually measured by circumference, whereas that of a wire rope is reckoned by diameter. Indeed a craft so old has its innumerable and recondite technical terms, but as with the different fibres used in manufacture, each has a purpose for which it is best suited. When this system of nomenclature is married to that of different fibres and their known qualities, the ropemaker's always fruity vocabulary is enriched by many permutations and combinations.

Within recent years the arrival of the synthetic fibres has immensely increased the range of ropes. Nylon was an American discovery, Terylene a British. They have some different properties but many in common. In common they are very much stronger, weight for weight, than the vegetable fibres, highly extensible and elastic. The strength of a nylon rope is in fact about twice that of a manila rope of the same size. These ropes, even after heavy strain, return almost to their original lengths after the load has been removed. They do not suffer from abrasion so much as the fibre ropes, abrasion merely creating a 'fuzz' that is really protective. Neither nylon nor Terylene is attacked by mildew or any other known bacterial pest; they—Terylene in particular —absorb very little water in marine use; and they are highly resistant to most chemicals to which they are likely to be exposed.

It is thus obvious that ropes or cord of synthetic fibre are peculiarly well-suited to lighter marine purposes such as fishing and yachting, but it is of much interest that not only the whaling men of the South Atlantic have come to prefer ropes of synthetic fibre for some of their

Part of one of the massive modern Gill Spinning Machines on which rope yarn is produced today. The 'Gills', at one of which the operator is working, tuck loose ends of fibre into the yarn, so giving a smoother finished yarn.

special purposes, but that, on some of the largest vessels afloat, these same fibres have found their true *métier*. In the meantime we see that the range of materials of this sort produced by The Gourock Ropework Company is almost fantastically varied. One feels that any woman would be happy in a ropework, so vast is the range of material, twists, textures and dyes—all the way down the scale from a towing hawser to a spool of horticulturalist's twine.

In 1920 The Gourock acquired the business and premises of the old Govan Ropeworks. Govan, once a proudly independent burgh, is now absorbed in the massive municipality of Glasgow. On the south bank of the Clyde, its river front is almost solid with shipyards and, especially in the days of sail, the Govan Ropeworks provided their considerable opportunities for local labour. Ropes are still made in quantity in Port Glasgow as we have seen, and in the historic, original ropewalk of the Port Glasgow Rope and Duck Company; but the works in Govan now form the largest rope-producing unit within The

Gourock organisation. A serious fire in October 1955 had at least its compensation in allowing the Company to lay out the Govan works for the even more modern and efficient manufacture of ropes and cordage. It deals with the raw materials, largely sisal, on their own account, but the rest is ropes and cords, without the complications of canvases and their many associated processes intervening. The Govan ropewalk, like a long section of the London Underground, runs to over 250 fathoms in length, almost certainly the longest covered ropewalk in the world, and it can turn out a rope or hawser of 200 fathoms or more; nearly one-quarter of a mile. Some 250 people, mostly women, find employment here, the apparently small total being the measure of the modern, mechanised nature of the plant.

This is the place in which the processes of ropemaking are seen to the layman's best advantage. The compact, fussy House machines are always turning out ropes of relatively small circumference; in that cavernous ropewalk they may be running up a hawser that could hold a battleship to her berth in a storm . . . As for that term 'House'—it is not that of an inventor or a patentee. It was so christened by the traditional ropelayers, who believed that a proper rope must be 'walk-laid'—that is, made only on a proper ropewalk and not in a mere four-square building.

It is in the stores at Govan that one sees most clearly the range of ropes produced by The Gourock from vegetable fibres. (They do not deal there with the synthetics.) Here is a wealth of ropes in all manner of materials and circumferences: ropes of nearly white sisal, whippy ropes of darker manila hemp, tarred ropes with the healthy smell of the sea about them; ropes sewn up for dispatch to the ends of the earth; ropes through which a customer has had a coloured yarn or his own marking tape, even coloured strands, embodied for his own trade purposes. Some parcels like great cheeses have been wrapped in bright tartan paper and then covered with polythene sheet. The North American fisherman likes it that way. Gaily coloured also are the large quantities of cordage that go to Canada to make, say, hauling ropes for toboggans, often confections of red, white and blue strands.

Govan produces quantities of coir rope as required. Coir is twisted from coconut fibre brought in from Ceylon, as roughly prepared by native labour. It used to be built up into very large towing springs for heavy marine purposes, such as the berthing of large ships; but today

At our Works in Govan are the longest Rope Railways in Europe. Here one of them, now equipped with the most modern ropemaking machinery following the serious fire of 1955, is seen laying-up a 9-strand cable.

General view of part of the present Govan Rope Store which was also earlier destroyed by fire.

the emphasis lies more perhaps with the fishing industry. And in Govan, in fact (as too in Port Glasgow), one sees the marriage of heavy ropes of vegetable fibre or synthetic material to the strong wire ropes produced in the Company's steel-wire ropeworks in Shettleston at the other end of Glasgow. The linking of wire and fibre in these springs allows the vegetable or synthetic material to provide in heavy towing or docking operations the elasticity the wire rope alone cannot give.

Wire ropes were made at Port Glasgow during the 1890's, but the manufacture seems to have lasted for only about five years, from 1893 until 1898. Some 40 years passed before The Gourock renewed its interest in this branch of the business. In 1938 it took over the long-established works of Archibald Thomson, Black & Company; and those who acted for The Gourock Ropework Company in that transaction like to recall that, when they went out to Shettleston to conclude the deal, the principal of the vendors, suffering from a bad cold, sat with a rug about his shoulders, his feet in a mustard bath! It was nevertheless a good deal for both parties concerned.

Thomson, Black & Company had been in the wire rope business almost from its beginning, and their standing was high in the British field of manufacture. The firm was founded in 1840, less than ten years after the first wire ropes were produced in viable form.

These were products of the genius and patience of Wilhelm Albert, a German interested in the mines of the Harz Mountains district. He worked and experimented over a period of some four years in the Caroline pit there and by 1834 was satisfied that he had discovered a rope more durable than one of traditional hemp. His rope, however, had fibre in its composition, and in the meantime an Englishman—George Wright Binks, foreman ropemaker at Woolwich Dockyard—had been working along the same lines. He faithfully followed the traditional fibre technique, and in 1835 created the first fine stranded wire rope produced in this country out of left-handed strands laid together right-handed. In 1838 the Admiralty sanctioned the use of steel wire ropes in H.M. ships and ordained that a number of them should be rigged with the new material: perhaps a unique example of swift decision by Their Lordships.

Starting up in the wire rope-making business in 1840, Thomson and Black were early in the field; their firm was the first of its kind in Scotland. They supplied an obviously growing demand, for the metal rope was an inevitable symbol of the Industrial Revolution. The improved steam engine was putting heavier and heavier stresses on its auxiliaries. Mines were being sunk deeper and deeper, ships were being built larger and heavier; machinery of all sorts was requiring the rope to take heavier stresses than vegetable fibres could stand with reasonable economy. Thus the making of steel wire rope, the nature of the raw material taken into account, became a branch of engineering, a precision job . . . and yet it remains in many of its basic aspects not so far separated from the ancient art of twisting ropes out of fibrous material.

You twist steel wire of various diameters into strands and you twist the strands into ropes: from any size from the fine, whippy material of a yacht's rigging to a wire for towing or mooring a huge ship or a monstrous steel cable for slipping an ocean-going vessel. The modern processes being highly mechanised, wire does not need to be handled along the vast length of the traditional ropewalk; it is wound on drums as it comes out of the machines in almost exactly the same way, in fact, as are fibre ropes made on House machines. The standard shipping types are normally made in two lengths, 90 and 120 fathoms respectively, but out Shettleston way The Gourock will, due notice given, make you a monstrous wire rope of 500 fathoms in length—more than half a mile of it. At the same time, any small trader—say, a builder wishing to renew the worn rope of a small crane in his back premises—can walk into the stores and buy just a few yards of the material he requires.

The steel wire ropemaker insists on the exact division of his provinces. He manufactures for marine purposes, and he manufactures for engineering purposes. Most ropes for maritime purposes are galvanised against corrosion; all those for engineering purposes are not galvanised but are, on the other hand, heavily lubricated. Many ropes on the list are of wire wound over a core of fibrous material, giving an additional degree of flexibility, and some types for special purposes have fibre twisted in with the steel wire. Where fibrous cores are used, very stringent standards of internal lubrication are observed.

It remains interesting that the wire ropemaker follows his cousin in the fibre rope business in using special terms for his 'lays'. He uses an Ordinary Lay, twisted to both right and left; for particular jobs he produces a Seale Lay or a Warrington Lay, each with its character and

Part of the thoroughly modern Steel Wire Rope Factory at Shettleston, Glasgow. The roof is of a shell construction in concrete and the floor is heated by concealed electrical elements—probably one of the first factories in Britain to be so treated.

virtues. His favourite is Lang's Lay, in which the wire in the strand runs in the same direction as the strands in the finished rope—streamlined all the way as it were. This brings it about that, instead of wearing across the line of its axis and becoming frayed, with tufts of wire showing along its length, the rope according to Lang's principle wears along the line of its axis and wears evenly.

But—and the technicalities are inevitable—Lang's Lay cannot have the field of wire ropemaking to itself. It serves admirably where both ends of the rope are anchored or where it travels in guides or on rails. It does not suit the freer purposes of shipping or general engineering. Here, to some extent, is reflected the anxiety that haunts the mind of wire rope users, The Factor of Safety.

This concerns his ropes in the place of manufacture itself. If a fibre rope breaks at any stage of its manufacture no great harm may be done, but if cold steel comes apart under overload, then the consequences are likely to be noisy and lethal. So, too, in manufacture. The long machines are heavily protected, and the men in charge use a

Usually known as 'snake' machines these heavy-duty stranders form and coil the individual strands ready for closing into steel wire rope. Stranders of this type accommodate up to 37 bobbins.

highly trained judgement in the control of the speed and tensile pulls of the machinery they supervise. (Relatively few women are employed in a wire ropework though their nimbler fingers serve in the creation of light ropes from fine-drawn wire.)

The wire rope, in fact, has almost always very heavy work to perform. Apart from its obvious uses in haulage, it has to take the burden of heavy hoisting in mines, in dredging equipment, in lifts nowadays working at high speeds, in excavating machinery and so on. All classes of Gourock wire rope are frequently tested to the point of destruction and are made to meet the highest standards of Lloyd's Register and other authorities.

The Gourock's works at Shettleston are old—and new. Strikingly new in its design and equipment is the addition to the old works put up in 1957. This is a soaring shell construction in concrete in six bays and without any obstructive pillars. The lighting is brilliant, the heating—one of the first factories ever to have it—is in the floor. New machines were installed and a few, duly overhauled, brought in from

127

the old building. It is thus in most ways a different sort of place from the traditional ropewalk; here labours the engineer at a precision job.

And yet the rope, even if built up from steel wire, carries history with it, a basic symbol of man's unending battle to manage the physical world about him. It somehow seems historically right that, when the principal of Archibald Thomson, Black & Company was handing over to the young representatives of The Gourock, he should have been wrapped in a rug and have had his feet in a mustard bath. He represented a hundred years of private enterprise and leadership in a new branch of a very ancient industry.

As for the charm and interest of the past, The Gourock Ropework Company returned in 1938 to a location it had abandoned exactly 70 years before. It will be recalled that the partners decided in 1841 to concentrate the manufacture of sailcloth in Port Glasgow and to set up, on the line of the Shaws Water in Greenock, a mill for the spinning and manufacture of jute goods. This venture apparently met with indifferent success, so that the mill was sold though the ropewalk was retained. Then, in 1868, the partners changed their minds again and disposed of the ropewalk as well, minuting their intention that 'the manufacture of the Company's goods would henceforth be carried on solely at Port Glasgow'.

If these shifts of policy within less than 30 years seem fickle, let it be remembered that the Birkmyres were operating in a tricky market, especially since the conflict as between the sailing ship and the steam ship was still far from being resolved. It has already been sufficiently shown that the Company has quite frequently shifted its emphases from one of its bases to another, often moving heavy machinery over long distances, but the explanation is always that changing conditions of trade dictated these peregrinations. This was the factor operating when The Gourock took over Greenock Ropeworks, Ltd., in 1938, thus returning to an original site on the Whinhill high above Port Glasgow's neighbouring town. The business title, Greenock Ropeworks Ltd., was retained, but the ropewalk was always referred to within the organisation as Whinhill, the hill that rises steeply behind the town of Greenock and above the railway line to Wemyss Bay and the Clyde coast.

This was a relatively small local business, until 1938 mainly in family hands, and within The Gourock organisation it was a young brother among the giants, so to speak. It produced its good share of the Company's vast output of ropes—mainly in sisal and manila, with two specialities in the form of soft hemp and sisal tow yarns, to be made up at Port Glasgow. Then, in June 1961, the Whinhill name again disappeared from the records. Once more in the interests of concentration it was disposed of to friendly rivals.

Thus, to recapitulate, The Gourock Ropework Company produces its ropes at three centres—one in the Port Glasgow area, two in Glasgow proper. Great ropes are still laid in the original ropework at Port Glasgow, and it is a striking observation that, in spite of the undoubted streamlining and modernisation of plant and technique, the *very same* ropewalk building which produced in Stevenson's day—and as shown in Paul's early print—still today and every day produces its share of The Gourock's great output. The large works at Govan deal exclusively in ropes on a major scale and spin their own yarn. Steel wire rope-making is concentrated in the modernised works at Shettleston.

Chapter IX

THE MAKING OF NETS

It is fascinating to speculate on the order in which man made his primary discoveries in the field of mechanics. There is the word of the archaeologists for it that the shards of fishing nets, dating from the Stone Age and cunningly knotted, have been discovered in Central Europe, a date that makes the parable of the loaves and fishes seem almost modern. There is the strange fact that the Eskimos, apparently isolated from the trends of early civilisation, worked out their own techniques of catching fish with nets made up of strands of hide. But it would also seem that the rope antedated the net, for it is unlikely that any net could be cast and hauled in, or even strung across a stream, without some sort of rope to anchor it.

So far as The Gourock Ropework Company is concerned, it came into the business of making nets relatively late in the day, having been content to concentrate for more than 100 years on the production of ropes, cordage and cloth. The Port Glasgow Rope and Duck Company was founded in 1736, The Gourock proper in 1777, and they were still serving a vast fishing fleet. The first historian of Greenock, Daniel Weir, in his 'History of the Town of Greenock' (1829) records that as late as 1757 'the take of herrings from the Garvel Perch to Finlayston Point, and even to Dumbarton Castle' was amazing. 'They are sold from eightpence to one shilling per hundred, for salting, and for the red-herring house at Gourock,' he adds, 'and the dealers in herrings come down here and salt up vast quantities in orange and lemon boxes, which they carry through the country on carts for sale'.

d-end of a Deep-sea Granton Trawl comes aboard. A remarkable photograph which has caught
dual drops of water, individual rays of sunlight and, in the angle of the cod-end, a fulmar in flight.

Probably both the Port Glasgow and the Gourock companies had their hands full with their rope and cloth manufactures and were content to leave net-making to a few scattered pockets of industry; and it may be borne in mind that the fishermen of the period and their womenfolk were skilled in making nets by hand. Certainly, The Gourock was not seriously interested in the net-making business until Henry Birkmyre III and his brother-in-law, R. G. Sommerville, took over the New Lanark mills and imported skilled operatives and machinery. They went far afield for their material, buying looms from places so remote as the fishing townlets of Caithness. They imported labour and machinery from the Isle of Man and other centres of the trade—places as far apart as Kilbirnie in Ayrshire and Bridport in Dorset; and with the latter town, as we shall see, The Gourock has still an interesting association.

There was some net-making at Port Glasgow itself towards the end of the 19th century, but it does not appear to have been extensive, and there seems no doubt that when in 1898 the partners bought an old mill in Lynedoch Street, Greenock, now The Gourock's chief net-making establishment, they were thinking more of the land than of the sea. (Again we encounter the shift of manufacturing emphasis that follows changing demand.) They intended to create here a factory for the production of binder twine, as we have seen. The self-binding reaping machine had crossed the Atlantic, and vast quantities of twine were required for the sheaves it could cut at what then seemed a fantastic speed. There was also the consideration, already quoted, that female labour was scarce in Port Glasgow and plentiful in Greenock. An accident of history completely changed the outlook within a year of the purchase going through.

The Lynedoch Street premises, though nowadays completely modernised, were old. Indeed, they had lain vacant for a while, occasionally used by the sugar refiners of Greenock for the storage of their raw materials. With the building The Gourock acquired a venerable bell. It bears the moulded legend—Le Solide, 1748—its only other decoration being a cross. The history of this bell has never been traced with certainty, but it may safely be assumed that it came out of one of the many French prizes brought into the Clyde during the Napoleonic wars. It no longer calls the folk to work. In 1940 or thereabouts, with air raids impending, it had to be taken down from its little belfry and replaced for warning purposes by klaxons. But it is lovingly preserved.

In the meantime, the emergency that switched Lynedoch Street away from the production of binder twine was the outbreak of the South African War. Providing the canvas out of its own resources, the War Office required vast quantities of the goods in which The Gourock had long specialised—from marquees by way of bell tents down to covers for mess-tins. This new branch of the organisation was therefore turned over to war work of great urgency, the operatives on piece-time during the emergency.

Probably a trophy of the Napoleonic Wars, this bell—bearing the inscription 'Le Solide, 1748'—used to be the Works bell at our Lynedoch Street Net Factory.

Fortunately, one of the veterans interviewed a few years ago could recall those hectic days clearly. He recorded that, apart from marquees and hospital tents, Lynedoch Street was expected to produce 750 bell tents each week: surely a staggering figure since most of the work was done by hand. The technique of manufacture was fairly simple. Roughly, a length of cloth was divided into ten rectangular pieces by a cutter under pressure. Each of these square pieces was then split from corner to corner by knife. It took 22 of these triangular panels plus a door-flap to make one bell tent, and a girl was expected to stitch nine tent-bodies in one day. The establishment worked a 10-hour day, and often enough the active sons of Henry Birkmyre III would be up to labour with their employees on this rush job. The piece-work rates provided heavy pay packets 60 years ago, but our witness, Mr McCartney, could say with feeling in his old age, 'It was very hard work'.

Fine social divisions were not unknown in the Lynedoch Street of those early days. It is recorded that the young ladies employed on the piece-work stitching of tents considered themselves so much an 'élite corps'—and, being paid the fabulous sum of more than 30 shillings a week, a distinct cut above their lesser fellow workers—that they all adopted wide-brimmed hats and white, starched blouses as a uniform of demarcation. Today, we should most likely call it a status symbol.

Mr McCartney rose to a position of importance at Lynedoch Street later on, and he provided a useful sketch of the transference of net-making capacity from New Lanark to Greenock once the South African War demands had been satisfied. It appears, however, that The Gourock's net-making activities were widely scattered before the concentration in Greenock was achieved. Apparently, three small factories in the Isle of Man and one at Bridport, all using hand looms, were kept going *in situ*. They were at first engaged in turning out mackerel and Dutch nets, the latter made of coarser yarn than the Scottish fisherman would tolerate. They then turned to finer nets for the Scottish drift-net fleets, and the goods were brought to Lynedoch Street for mounting and barking—that is, steeped in anti-rot fluids; and it is interesting that men were brought over from Man to do this work and, no doubt, teach their craft to a new generation.

It took a long time to concentrate the net-making branch of the business in Greenock; New Lanark was a rival over many years. When the small factories in Man and at Bridport were closed, the hand-powered looms were first sent to New Lanark, and then, in 1910, they were moved to Greenock, which already had equipment of the kind. So it was with the powered looms that were duly installed—looms of the Zang type in New Lanark, looms of another in Greenock, the latter intended mainly for the production of herring drift nets. This division of effort lasted until 1930, when the Zang looms from Lanark went to Greenock, the whole of the power loom equipment concentrated in the latter place. In the meantime, looms for weaving cloth had been sent overland to Robert Owen's old kingdom from both Greenock and Port Glasgow. Thus we know with certainty that net-making was concentrated at Lynedoch Street in 1930 while New Lanark definitely went over to making cotton cloth in the same year: a milestone in The Gourock's history.

The power loom for net-making is a monstrous contraption. It is of huge bulk and length, since it has to produce lengths of netting up to about 35 feet in breadth and from 100 to 200 yards in length. It disappoints the layman in that, behind the long rows of its steel teeth,

Ohls Double-knot Loom used exclusively on synthetic nets, principally nylon.

one cannot see how the twine being fed into its maw from the whirling spindles is miraculously knotted. Hereby hangs a tale.

When the first machine-made nets were put on the market in the early years of this century the Scottish fisherman, at least, thought poorly of them, and sales tended to drop. The fisherman is admittedly a conservative man, but there was good sense behind the objection. The power loom made its sheet-bend knots forming the mesh at angles differing from those in the hand-braided net, and it was the fisherman's experience that if a power-produced net had to be cut for repair it was apt to unravel. Meanwhile, for the record, Mr McCartney testified that a goodly number of female hand-braiders were still at work at Lynedoch Street in his time, deftly wielding the tools of their trade— the braiding needle and the gauge of the mesh being produced. The number has declined to a mere handful, but their special skill is still required for the fortification of the huge nets that now go out from Greenock to all the oceans of the world.

The story of hand braiding at Greenock is a rather odd one on the human side. In 1922 only about a dozen girls were so employed at Lynedoch Street, but this number rose so rapidly to 90 or thereabouts, making trawl nets by hand, that the braiding department at Hull was closed down. Then, during and after the Second World War, like any shift of feminine fashion, the number of hand braiders started to decline; and in spite of efforts to build up the works staff on this side, the Greenock girls would not play, and much of the work was transferred back to Hull and to Milford Haven.

The fisherman's conservatism, a valuable quality, had to be overcome again when the synthetic fibres were introduced. He liked the good old-fashioned net of vegetable fibre barked brown, its upper edges supported in the water by those glass balls some of us must have picked up as trophies of the seashore. Here was another prejudice that had to be broken down.

A place where nets are made on modern lines is a most attractive place: again one to charm any woman with her love of fine fabrics and colours. It is also infinitely less noisy than places in which cloth is woven. It is a pleasure to see how the very fine filament supplied by the manufacturers—as light as gossamer but in fact very strong—is spun to make thread, then the thread spun to make the twine that goes to the looms to be fashioned into nets—nets of mesh suited to catching

These two photographs, taken over 6,000 miles apart, show a remarkable similarity and a remarkable contrast. The first shows the double braiding of a Granton Trawl Cod-end at our Lynedoch Street Net Factory, and the other, Trawl Cod-ends being braided by native girls in our Net Factory at Elsies River, South Africa.

mature fish by the gills, nets of fine mesh that must hopelessly enclose all creatures, large or small, trapped within them; strong nets for the salmon fisheries of British Columbia as well as of the British Isles; nets for the protection of growing fruit or the support of sweet peas; nets for protection of forestries and farmlands; nets for the safe carriage of explosives. There are nets for cricket, football, lawn tennis. Now and again the producer of an amateur dramatic society appears to buy a length of fine netting which, treated with aluminium paint, passes as chain mail in a costume play.

The range is endless, but it is the note of bright colour in the synthetic twines that catches the lay eye most emphatically. Today, the bright orange of the polythene filament predominates, but one may glimpse here and there bundles of netting in a variety of shades.

One supreme end-product of the Lynedoch Street works is the Gourock Wing Trawl Net. This is of a design evolved from patient study of international fishing techiques and from the results of experiment, with the practical fisherman contributing his views. The Wing

Trawl is a lengthy piece of construction—130 feet overall on the average —and to see it being made up is to be reminded of the processes of boatbuilding. The skilled men who produce them are working (as even the wire experts at Shettleston might admit) on a sort of engineering job. The mouth of the great orange belly of the net must be supported by strong ropes of combined sisal and wire, a product of Shettleston. Then it must be accurately rigged to work over the ocean floor, and then it must be buoyed with equal accuracy for its upper edges to float high, with the mouth wide open. Finally, the cod-end—that is the elongated bag into which the catch is ultimately driven—is strongly fortified and, in turn, protected from damage on the sea bed by the chafer which encloses it with still heavier netting. The observant eye will also see that the length of orange netting is divided into panels, so to call them, by narrow strips of black or coloured twine. This is a device, the product of experience, whereby any damaged area of a net can be easily identified and isolated for repair.

The products of Lynedoch Street go all over the world—to West Africa, East Africa, New Zealand, Canada, Australia, Iceland, the West Indies, South Africa, Ceylon, the Bermudas and the Seychelles. The Wing Trawl, besides being an increasing favourite with the British and Irish fisherman, is in demand from New Zealand, Canada and West Africa. And there are special nets for shrimps, special nets for pilchards—the whole range a lesson in ecology. But now we turn to see how the output from Greenock is supplemented from certain bases far away.

Any fishing net is a delicate piece of goods, continually subjected to hazard, and when The Gourock Ropework Company first went into this branch of textile working, with New Lanark as the base of operations, it was obvious that goods bearing the 'Gourock' brand must be available where the fleets were most busily at work. The herring had departed from the upper Firth of Clyde, and the fleets on the lower reaches were diminishing. In any event, the Clyde and the West Highlands alone could not absorb the output of The Gourock's net-works, whether at New Lanark or in Greenock. The net had to follow the fisherman, and we have seen that factories at Peel in the Isle of Man and at Bridport in Dorset were taken over. Stocks of nets made in Scotland could easily be stored at strategic points, but it was clearly desirable that facilities for braiding and repair should be available at

One of the most successful nets ever, a Gourock Wing Trawl is shown going into action off an Ayr boat in the lower Clyde Estuary.

all the larger centres of the fishing industry, and the most obvious of these was one or other of the great fishing ports of East Anglia, the huge fleets attracted annually to the prolific expanses of the North Sea.

It appears that The Gourock first established at least a store and sail-loft at Yarmouth during the latter half of the 19th Century, but this centre of gravity—although retained until recently—shifted its emphasis to Lowestoft in 1887. The move was successful, and a large number of local girls found employment in the branch.

The Lowestoft outpost remains a valuable unit of the larger organisation, and it has made a name for itself through its sail-loft in a specialised field. Showmen and other users of fairgrounds abound in that quiet and prosperous part of Old England, and the loft at Lowestoft is large enough and sufficiently well equipped to have established a valuable line in the many sorts of canvas goods these specialists require.

The cloth is manufactured in Scotland, but Lowestoft will run you up anything from the walls of a coconut shy to the elaborate tilt of a Dodgem arena. Its connections with the great showman families are intimate. The Bostocks have relied on its services, and it once produced a great tent for Lord John Sanger's Circus, this involving the use of 3,000 yards of handsewn canvas. The Lowestoft masterpiece was the production for the Japanese Government after the First World War of an airship shed requiring 6,000 yards of canvas; and through two wars it has been a prolific supplier of goods in Birkmyre's Cloth.

The chain of branch establishments round the coasts of Britain is now comprehensive. To take the fishing side alone, there are branches at Aberdeen, Cardiff (including Milford Haven), Fleetwood, Hull, Lowestoft, North Shields and Plymouth. Heavy stocks of gear are carried at each depôt, but at all excepting Cardiff and North Shields the arts of net braiding and repair are practised by skilled workers. The Aberdeen establishment, taken over from a local firm in 1904, has some features all its own. We have seen that it makes up salmon nets manufactured in Greenock—those vast nets we see stretched between uprights in coastal waters near the approaches to the great salmon rivers—but its workers produce great lengths of fishing lines on machines specially installed to serve the regional branches of the fishing industry: those required by the Greatline fishing fleet and cotton twine for the Bagnet fishing of salmon.

The Gourock Ropework Company has many ramifications overseas

Winter seas on the fishing grounds do not encourage the chicken-hearted. If it is not up to standard it breaks—and that goes for men as well as for gear.

and these will be accounted for. In the special department of nets, however, its one effective manufacturing centre outside Great Britain is in South Africa, at Elsies River on the Cape Flats nine miles from Cape Town. The establishment of the company's position in the southern parts of Africa was not uncomplicated by war and politics, as well as by the vast distances of travel involved, but The Gourock's pioneers in this field worked so well that it became desirable after the Second World War to produce on the spot the nets required by the great fishing fleets operating up and down the African coasts, and on the great lakes of the interior. A good site, with room to expand, was secured in the industrial district of Elsies River, and in 1947 a modern factory was completed.

This was a period in which shipping difficulties abounded, and it took time to train native girls in the craft of hand braiding, quick and eager learners though they were. When the power looms arrived in Cape Town at length the native labour force had to be trained all over again in the handling of these mechanical monsters. Everything was in order by the end of 1948, however, and the coastal fisherman could get from the new Gourock works in South Africa all he required in the way of nets manufactured at Elsies River. The reader with an eye for geography will note that Cape Town is a half-way house between Britain and Australia, and that the urgent requirements of the latter market could be supplied from the South African base.

Chapter X

THE GOUROCK OVERSEAS

It is known that some of the younger Birkmyre partners of The Gourock Ropework Company travelled extensively during the latter half of the 19th century, making and maintaining contacts, exploring potential markets and generally showing the flag. No exact records of these expeditions have survived, and it is reasonable to surmise that these emissaries from Port Glasgow were largely concerned with the inspection of agencies and the appointment of new agencies in likely places. The establishment of important branches and even manufacturing bases outside Scotland was still to come.

We know that, even before they sold out to The Gourock, the Port Glasgow Rope and Duck Company maintained stores, at least, in

143

Liverpool and London; and that that in London developed into an important sail-loft, still active. At the same time, the London establishment was more important as an agency in the citadel of British commerce, especially in the days when London river carried a great traffic of sailing ships and shipbuilding was still a lively industry on the Thames. We shall never know who originated the idea, but it was through London that the first substantial move overseas was made. This was towards South America.

The London office was for many years managed by one, Robert Young, trained in Port Glasgow. There are few who can now remember him, but the records indicate that he was a popular man, and that he enjoyed a long, active and useful life. London Manager he may have been nominally, but for many years towards the end of last century he was The Gourock's chosen representative sent far afield to open up new branches, engage and train native staff, and remain in charge until the new establishment was on its feet. His first assignment was to Buenos Aires.

The Gourock's offices in Buenos Aires.

Young went out to South America as a mere selling agent in the first place, making connections with traders of various nationalities. It seems, however, that he was shrewdly impressed by the possibilities of the Argentine Republic. Buenos Aires was already a large port; railways were being built, and a lively eye could see that the development of ranching and agriculture in the hinterland was creating a market for cloth, while the country's growing exports of meat involved an increasing tonnage of shipping. With the approval of the partners Robert Young returned to Buenos Aires in 1888 and opened an office in the Calle Mexico, 273, in due course handing this and an already good trade to the care of George H. Clarke from the Liverpool branch office.

This outpost prospered, though the goods it dispensed had to cross the Atlantic oceans from Scotland. It dealt at first mainly in manila ropes, sail cloths of cotton and flax, and Birkmyre's Cloth. As agriculture developed, the demand for covers and sewing twines steadily increased. There was even a good trade in cotton ducks for the making of *alpargatas*, the canvas shoes with plaited fibre soles that are still used by a majority of the native workers on the various development schemes. It was thus not long before it became clear that this Buenos Aires branch should enjoy larger manufacturing facilities than the mere capacity to sew covers and tents by hand.

Robert Young had certainly opened up an exciting market in the developing continent. In due course branches were set up in Brazil, Chile and Peru, each coping with the lively demands of expansion, each providing young men from Britain with opportunities of adventure both in trading and social experience. The trade depression from the mid 20's onwards in South America led to the closing of those outlying branches, with the exception of Buenos Aires, but they were valuable outposts of the advance The Gourock was then making to extend its trading frontiers.

It was in 1906 that, at the earnest recommendations of the men on the spot in Buenos Aires, the partners in Port Glasgow agreed to send out sewing machines from home. With them went John Cormie of the office staff (later to become a Director in Port Glasgow), Tommy Andrews, an engineer, and Robert Hopkins, a sail-loft foreman. The manager in Buenos Aires at the time was still George H. Clarke from the Liverpool office. He was 40 years in the Argentine before retiring

J. G. Mackenzie, pioneer of The Gourock's South African organisation, camps beside his small Cape Cart in the veldt about the turn of the century. It seems incredible that in such a short span of years so large a South African and Rhodesian organisation should have grown from such humble—and physically dangerous—journeys of exploration.

in 1928, but he had seen by then his organisation grow to be a power in that South American land.

The tutorial team from Port Glasgow spent the best part of a year in the Argentine, teaching native workers how to manage the machines —and learning how to do so in Spanish. It was Mr Cormie's task to instruct young Argentinians in the intricacies of office routine within a specialised industry. A productive organisation, if with limited resources, was growing up nicely when, towards the end of the First World War, the branch got notice to move from the rented premises in which it had set up its cover factory.

This seemed at the time to be a setback. It proved to be a blessing in disguise. Assured again by the enthusiasm of their representatives in Buenos Aires, the directors in Scotland authorised them to look around for a site on which a cover factory and store could be built, with room

146

for possible expansion. By 1924 the Argentine branch was in possession of a roomy new factory fronted by an office block of pleasing design.

And still the business grew. It is cutting a long though very interesting story short to report that, by 1930, the enthusiasts in Buenos Aires had persuaded the Board in Port Glasgow that they could not always meet the demands for ropes out of stock, and that they should be allowed to produce at least a limited range of ropes on the spot from yarns sent over from Scotland. The machinery was planned in the first place to produce ropes of only 4-inch circumference at the most, but the day soon came when natural development and extensions allowed The Gourock in the Argentine to turn them out up to 11-inch circumference—far beyond the capacity of any rival concern within the Republic.

In spite of the vagaries of South American politics the Buenos Aires branch has enjoyed friendly and profitable relations with the departments of the Argentine Government. Leaps and bounds—the old phrase well describes its progress. The outpost in South America achieved full status in 1949, when it was granted the capital to extend once again and set up its own fibre-spinning plant, thus becoming an independent and self-contained factory of large productive power. It is a pleasant fact that the circus *motif* recurs in this chapter of The Gourock's story. The Argentinians are a gay people, and the Buenos Aires establishment has long been in the business of supplying show tents and marquees. Its masterpiece was a Big Top for Sarrasani, the German showman then touring South America. This required 10,000 yards of top quality white Birkmyre's Cloth and three tons of tarred hemp cordage.

Today, Buenos Aires branch can claim another unique distinction in the Gourock organisation. It was the first overseas branch—and is today one of only two—at which proofing of cloths by the proprietary Birkmyre process is carried out.

As we have seen, the Port Glasgow Rope and Duck Company was dealing extensively with the American Colonies before the Revolution, and it was natural that, after that event, The Gourock should resume its dealings with North America through Canada. Great quantities of materials manufactured in Scotland had been exported through agents to serve the fishing industries of the Maritime Provinces and the growing needs of the prairie farmers, but it was not until 1903 that an independent branch of The Gourock was set up in Montreal.

Once again, Robert Young was on the spot to pioneer the enterprise. He took premises in the down-town business section of the city, and Herbert Stewart was sent over from Head Office to be manager.

Montreal headquarters of The Gourock.

Young's shrewdest move, however, was to enlist and train as traveller a young Irish-Canadian, Harry W. Palmer, who had the valuable gift of speaking fluent French. He did not retire until 1948, after 45 years of service with The Gourock, and in that time he had firmly planted the Port Glasgow flag over a wide area of a vast country.

The range of Mr Palmer's travels provides a good measure of the effort required of any of The Gourock's representatives in a large territory overseas. During his first year he established accounts in all cities and towns as far west from Montreal as Sault Ste. Marie. His regular beat was over the whole Province of Quebec, then Nova Scotia and New Brunswick. In each year he made two side-trips to Boston and Gloucester, Mass., and to Newfoundland. He was called upon to train new hands, and one of these, his brother Herbert, took over the vast expanse of territory between Toronto and British Columbia.

In spite of the many difficulties created by travelling over such vast areas, The Gourock's business in Canada so expanded that it was found necessary in 1920 to move the original Montreal office to much larger premises. Montreal, like Buenos Aires, comprised a manufacturing unit, if of limited capacity, and the headquarters of a selling organisation that yearly achieved the miracle of covering the enormous territory between the Maritimes and British Columbia. On the outbreak of the Second World War supplies of goods from Scotland dried up, and Montreal reorganised itself as far as possible to become a main supplier of the Royal Canadian Navy. Quantities of Carley floats, lifebelts, ship's fenders, awnings and service covers were turned out, and the fitting-out of many frigates and other ships of war built in eastern Canada was entrusted to this vigorous Canadian offspring. During these war years another sail-loft was set up at the naval base of Halifax, Nova Scotia, and was kept working day and night for five years until 1946. Another was opened in due course at Lunenburg, a traditional home of rich cookery, but it proved to be too far from the centre of things, and a return to Halifax was ordained in 1953. There the Maritime office of The Gourock remains.

For a year or two just before and after the end of the war the factory in Montreal turned out trawl nets, but when British industry got back into its stride after the emergency it became obvious that these Canadian manufactures could not compete in price with goods produced in Scotland, and the machinery was put into cold storage. On the other hand, an amalgamation with Bridport Industries, Ltd., of Bridport, Dorset, has reinforced the netting connection. Bridport Industries produce commercial fishing lines, sporting nets of all kinds, hemp salmon nets and nylon netting, and this specialised output interlocks conveniently with The Gourock's standard goods, although The Gourock still supplies its own nets to Canada.

The Canadian company is thus now Gourock-Bridport, Ltd.* Its business in Montreal is largely of a marine nature, though with a tidy trade in industrial and sporting goods, and there is also a lot of work to be done for Canada's two railway systems. The Nova Scotia branch, so greatly concerned with the provision of gear for the fishermen of the Maritimes, is kept busy at its headquarters in Halifax, whilst through new premises in Toronto westward consolidation continues.

If North America was obviously a good potential market for Gourock products from the beginning, Australasia was equally so. The development of Australia and New Zealand was perhaps patchy, but the distances involved were great. As early as 1902 The Gourock had a place of its own in Sydney. Until then, the Far East and Australasia had been covered—and it must have been in a somewhat sketchy fashion—by Tom Black, a New Lanark lad who had had his final training at Head Office in Port Glasgow. (He is still remembered by a few old hands as a man of agreeable nature and immaculate attire.) It was probably on his recommendation that a branch in Sydney was opened, with Mr J. G. McColl from Port Glasgow in charge.

The trading difficulties that faced Mr McColl were formidable. Competition from other countries was keen. But Australia had already been absorbing satisfactory quantities of The Gourock's products, especially in the form of the cotton and flax qualities of Birkmyre's Cloth. In fact, 'Birkmyre' had become a synonym for proofed canvas; in the backblocks any tarpaulin was just a 'Birkmyre'. This was pleasing in one sense, but it allowed producers of inferior goods virtually to infringe a copyright, and the Company was forced to take steps to protect its own good name and that of its high quality products.

The trade within Australia always has its problems for the British producer. The sheer unpredictability of Australian weather, drought or flood, is alone a chronic worry; and it is a very large country. There was for a time an established branch at Brisbane, Queensland, but it

* Since this history was written, a further merger has now altered the name to Gourock-Bridport-Gundry Ltd.

150

was latterly found most convenient to concentrate the business in the regions where the secondary native industries were being established, and by 1940 two factories for making up cloth were set up in Sydney and Melbourne respectively. The site of the original Sydney branch had to be abandoned in 1952, and while an office was duly opened in the city centre, excellent accommodation for manufacture and storage was found in the suburb of Concord, and there, as in Melbourne, the work of The Gourock proceeds steadily though within a set of admittedly difficult conditions.

For the Gourock the situation in Australia became more difficult after the Second World War. Conscious of a growing sense of nationhood, well aware of its strategic importance in relation to South-East Asia, and with its own industries increasing in variety and expanding, the Australian Government felt obliged to impose import duties—and quotas—on goods manufactured abroad. In particular, a native industry in ropes and cloths had developed rapidly, and over the years it became more and more heavily protected. This led to the large decision, taken in 1960, that the demand for canvas in the expanding Australian market must be met, at least in part, by on-the-spot production and that The Gourock must build big to keep the flag flying high under the Southern Cross.

A suitable site was found at Seven Hills, some miles from Sydney, and there, as this History is being written, a large new factory is going up: the ground acquired allowing for the doubling of its size if need be. This factory will be devoted entirely to the manufacture of Birkmyre's Cloth for the Australian market. Right through to the waterproofing and rotproofing of these cloths, their production will be by the same processes and on similar plant to that in Scotland; and key personnel will go out from Port Glasgow to start it all working and remain to run it as long as necessary. The scheme is large enough to include the setting up of a control laboratory, and the sales staff will move out from Sydney to the new citadel.

This factory will operate under The Gourock's Australian subsidiary, The Birkmyre Canvas Company (Pty.), Ltd. This company is distinct from Gourock Ropes and Canvas, Ltd., which operates in New Zealand as well as in Australia; and, of course, in the Argentine.

The partners of The Gourock first opened up close communication with New Zealand by appointing a resident representative in

The new factory at Seven Hills, Sydney, referred to on the preceding page. Now complete and in production, it was opened by Australia's Prime Minister, the Rt. Hon. Sir Robert Menzies.

Wellington—again the ubiquitous Mr Tom Black. This Wellington branch, however, was under the jurisdiction of that in Sydney, Australia, and it was not until 1920, and after Black had resigned his position, that Head Office decided there should be an established branch and warehouse in Wellington.

The Gourock's trade in those far-flung islands is largely in canvases, proofed and unproofed. New Zealand has no native canvas industry but competition, from Australia in particular, does exist. The New Zealand Government has been obliged latterly to restrict imports, not to exclude the U.K. product, but solely to obtain a balance of payments. This is, in fact, a wholly typical example of the sort of problem that continually afflicts the overseas sales department of any large manufacturing concern. Ours is a world changing at fantastic speed. A small war, a shift of regional politics—and a whole department of reliable trade can be jeopardised. The Gourock's men in the branches overseas must develop, along with balanced judgement and intimate knowledge of local conditions, an exquisite sensibility. Who would care, at this moment of writing, to guess the likely trends of trade in Africa, for instance?

The Gourock Ropework Company ventured into South Africa in an organised way some years before it approached Australia.

Two men, William Cuthbert and J. G. Mackenzie, went out in 1897 and set up shop in a rented office and a store in Port Elizabeth, then the commercial centre of the country, and the reader will remember that this was before the South African War. The way of these pioneers was not easy at first; they had to travel, canvass and explore, riding with their samples in Cape carts over wide areas of country, of which the commercial possibilities had not then been accurately estimated. It appears that Cuthbert explored and exploited the regions northwards of Port Elizabeth, reaching as far as Beira in Portuguese territory and returning through Southern Rhodesia, then virgin country. In another picturesque but uncomfortable Cape cart Mackenzie pioneered the Cape Province and the Orange Free State. Both kept their shrewd eyes on the Johannesburg region and the developing mining industry about it.

The war of 1899-1902, its memories still affecting the Common-wealth, might be thought to have been fatal, but the importance of Cape Town as a British base in fact stimulated The Gourock's trade in cloth—just as that same war put Lynedoch Street on its feet through the demand for tents—and in 1899 Cuthbert and Mackenzie were empowered to take temporary premises in the city under Table Moun-tain. Shortly thereafter they bought the site on which the offices of the branch still stand.

The ultimate British victory steadied the situation in the country, and The Gourock started to spread. Branches were opened at Johannes-burg, Durban, East London and Bloemfontein; and in due course that in Johannesburg became the head office of the organisation in South Africa—Birkmyre House. More recently, the expansion of gold mining in the Orange Free State dictated the acquisition of a site at Welkom, the headquarters of the industry. Thus with the net factory at Elsies River already accounted for, The Gourock's stake in the future of South Africa, whatever that may be in political terms, is substantial.

Meanwhile, as the situation within the Union of South Africa became more stable from the manufacturer's point of view, the Rhod-esias were opening up to trade. William Cuthbert had discovered their potentialities at an early stage, and when the time was ripe branches were set up in Bulawayo, Salisbury and N'dola. The registered office of Gourock Ropes & Canvas (Rhodesia), Ltd., is in Salisbury. (This company is a subsidiary of Gourock Ropes and Canvas (Africa), Ltd., with headquarters in Johannesburg.) The student of commerce will again observe how cautiously the British-based firm must proceed to conform with the regulations of the newer countries.

The Gourock has no branch or registered subsidiary in East Africa, but that territory—designated as 'Head Office territory'—along with Zanzibar and Mauritius, has been worked over for a long time past. The official agents there, Messrs Smith, Mackenzie & Co., Ltd.—so closely associated with the British India Steam Navigation Company— have held the fort for many years, their efforts fortified frequently by visits from travellers sent out from home or from South Africa. Now a resident representative of The Gourock uses the Smith, Mackenzie offices in Nairobi as his headquarters.

He has wide territories to cover. Things in Kenya have perhaps not been expanding as rapidly as in Tanganyika and Uganda, but the power and mineral developments in all three countries require more and more Birkmyre goods. Climatic conditions in that part of the world are very sore on textiles, but The Gourock's tarpaulins have for years been specified as standard equipment for railways, harbours and other local Government enterprises.

Africa is a very large continent, and its politics are complicated and likely to remain so. The nature of The Gourock's representation in the Dark Continent provides coverage of the huge area in a remarkable degree of completeness, however. Roughly, the South African and Rhodesian subsidiaries can competently meet the needs of the territories from the line of the Congo southwards to the Cape. The East African unit covers the developing areas between the coast and Uganda, the islands of Zanzibar and Mauritius, soon possibly, territories still farther west. As for the territories to the North—the Sudan, Ethiopia, Egypt, and so on—it is obvious that these are most easily serviced from Europe across the Mediterranean. A network of agencies, with a good deal of help from the aeroplane, render that problem of representation and administration relatively simple.

Although The Gourock has no subsidiary of its own in West Africa, it has long had connection with the markets there; but it has been one

This is 'Birkmyre House', Port Elizabeth. It is typical of the modern premises The Gourock now has all over South Africa and Rhodesia.

of the characteristics of these markets that much of their commerce is carried out indirectly, through the offices of West African importers in Liverpool, Manchester and London. Certainly representatives of the firm have from time to time visited these areas from Head Office, but the wind of change now blowing there is leading more and more to the establishment of direct on-the-spot agencies, the pattern already so familiar elsewhere.

There are six branches of The Gourock in the Union of South Africa, three in Rhodesia. Add the much larger number of agencies scattered throughout the continent and along its coasts, and the coverage is seen to be complete—necessary in these times of intense competition and austere import control. What it takes to keep a large British manufacturing concern in the market is best realised from the map of The Gourock's positions throughout the world: a vast organisation built up over many years of geographical and economic study, of adventure and applied enthusiasm in the selling of quality goods.

The story of The Gourock overseas would make a book by itself, the ventures and adventures studied as romantic aspects of British industrial history. Such men as Robert Young and Tom Black in several regions, as Cuthbert and Mackenzie in South Africa, were of the pioneering breed. They must often have encountered positive physical danger, they surely knew weariness and isolation and they encountered resistance and experienced frustration. So it is to this day with any young man sent out to an overseas branch, however comfortable his passage and his accommodation. He has almost always to adjust himself to an unfamiliar set of social conditions and conventions. It is the first part of his duty that, with the greatest discretion, he must watch and learn, feeling a political situation with sensitive antennae, smelling out a potential market from afar, watching day in, day out, the jumps of currencies and the antics of political groups. He knows that, away back in Port Glasgow, in the Export Sales Department, keen men with statistical minds are watching the results of his work, for more than 40 per cent of The Gourock's output is sold overseas.

Not overseas, but over the Border, the company made a foray in October 1945. This was the acquisition, as a wholly owned subsidiary, of the old firm of J. Lomax & Sons (Bolton), Ltd. This company had been formed in 1849, and its premises and equipment were admittedly backward. It is no longer so: an entirely new building in the modern idiom, new machinery, lighting, heating and so on have worked miracles, and in this Lancashire subsidiary The Gourock has a useful auxiliary for the production of covers, mill-bags, news-bags, sunblinds and such specialised articles as searchlight covers. This subsidiary still trades under the old Lomax family name.

The 'news scoop' picture of its day—the 'Queen Elizabeth' in the wartime grey that was to be her only garb until after the war, secretly noses down the River Clyde for the very first time to start her formidable war record.

Chapter XI

THE GOUROCK AT WAR

Modern war is a grievous break in the affairs of a large manufacturing concern. It means direction by Government and tight control of raw materials. This in its turn interrupts the production of those goods the manufacturer has evolved as the staples of his trade. It means unresting improvisation and a nearly unbearable strain on the men in the higher executive levels. Fatigue becomes an important industrial factor, wearing out the management and, through the demands of the Services, calling for wearing hours of work from a depleted labour force only dubiously skilled. "War profiteer" was a coinage of the First World conflict; in the Second, taxation of draconic severity made the phrase seem silly.

It is all taken as read nowadays; there has been so much writing and talking on the subject; but a younger generation that did not live as adults through the emergency should know that it was a ghastly period in the history of this country. The black out turned cities, towns and villages into dangerous mysteries, if not infernoes after sunset; for years on end few men and women in the United Kingdom could rest with complete composure, the inner ear always straining for the wailing of the air raid sirens, for the chilling, undulating drone of attacking enemy aircraft. Restrictions and shortages rendered food and drink scarce and monotonous; the annual holiday became nearly an impossibility. . . . It has all been told often enough before, Goodness knows! but to look back on those days is to wonder that such a large concern as The Gourock Ropework Company could keep going with an efficiency that allowed it to make a large contribution to the war effort and still leave it with the strength to face the huge task of post-war reorganisation.

On the scale of modern war the dealings of The Gourock with the authorities during the South African War seem almost comic. As we have seen, they had to work very hard in the Lynedoch Street works to get out the supplies of bell tents the War Office required, but that little emergency of the day before yesterday was hardly the desperate struggle for mere survival that was to come fifteen years later and, in a still more desperate form, in 1939. This history has been able to quote a few memories of the South African crisis, timeously recorded a few years ago from the lips of one or two very old people. Even in 1960, however, coherent survivors of the 1914–18 period were becoming thin on the ground, and memories of crisis had not, as in the case of those who worked in industry during the 1939–45 period, been sharpened by long exposure to the threats of invasion and bombing.

If the Government required bell tents by the thousand for the war in South Africa, it requires little imagination to estimate its appetite for stores in 1914. For one thing, the Royal Navy had never been so powerful, and its demands for ropes, cordage and cloth were insatiable. For another, the land campaigns—even that in Flanders, to some extent—were to be conducted from tented bases, those in Egypt, Mesopotamia and India forming canvas towns, almost cities. The development of the war itself produced fresh demands; the new science of camouflage, for example, requiring vast quantities of nets and cloth.

If anything pressed with particular weight on such concerns as The Gourock during the 1914–18 War it was the maintenance of a sufficient labour force and the preservation of skilled departmental management. Perhaps only those who lived through both periods as adults realise fully the differences in the public approaches to the conflicts. Nineteen hundred and fourteen released a torrent of volunteer enthusiasm, and specialised industry suffered until ways and means were found of combing the Forces for skilled men and returning them to their jobs. (Even so, too many valuable craftsmen were lost through the national inexperience of man management.) By 1939 the attitudes had changed completely. Government had done something towards the direction of labour, and most young men knew that the certainty of conscription must check their patriotic impulses—not that the rush of spirited lads to get into the more dangerous branches of the Services could be halted.

As for 1914–18, however, The Gourock suffered its chief loss of man-power through the compulsive volunteering of the period, and through the mobilisation of quite a number of men already enlisted in the Territorial Army units of the region. There was only compensation in the fact that the Women's Services in that first German war were but sketchily developed—that is, as compared with the brilliant and brave female formations of the second German war—and that a reasonably adequate pool of female labour was available in the Port Glasgow–Greenock area throughout. On the managerial side John Birkmyre II held high rank in the Port Glasgow Company of the Royal Garrison Artillery, but he was getting on in years, and it was more important in the national interest to keep him in direction of The Gourock's vital affairs than to post him to a fretful vigil behind his guns on some remote coastal site. His elder son, Henry Birkmyre III, took his place within the formation, serving as an officer of Garrison Gunners throughout the period of hostilities. So in due course, during 1939–45, the latter's son, the fourth John, continued the tradition as an officer in the Royal Artillery. ·

To resume: the business of any government that sees war as a possibility of the near future is to accumulate stocks of raw materials. The outbreak of war in 1914 had long been foreseen as almost inevitable; the crisis of 1939 came upon Britain more suddenly, however, and for a variety of reasons. Rightly or wrongly, the Baldwin Government

The last wartime convoy to cross the Atlantic anchored between the Tail o' the Bank and the anti-submarine boom linking Dunoon and the mainland.

had long declined to admit the threat represented by Hitler. Pacifist feeling throughout the United Kingdom was widespread. If many shrewd observers perceived what was brewing in the Third Reich, the national mood was to take Hitler and his rantings as a sort of continental joke in bad taste. Then Austria and Czechoslovakia were overwhelmed; and then Munich and a feverish digging of trenches brought the people to a sense of the crisis that was to bring sudden death from the air to a lot of simple people in the apparently remote Clydeside town of Port Glasgow and to involve the directors of its chief manufacturing concern in years of abrasive anxiety.

No doubt The Gourock Ropework Company stood high on Government lists of prime producers of essential war materials. No doubt the planners had had time, even during the short year of grace between Munich and the attack on Poland, to work out their allocations of raw materials. The outcome was a blow to a venerable firm that had prospered by virtue of its adherence to very high standards. While there were substantial stocks of manila hemp in the country for the manufacture of ropes, for instance, it was at once laid down by Government order that all ropes, even if ordered as manila, should be diluted, so to speak, by the use of sisal fibre to the tune of 33⅓ per cent. It was not very long before the proportion was changed to 50 per cent manila and 50 per cent sisal, and not long again before the permissible proportion of manila fell to 25 per cent against 75 per cent sisal. Finally, the pure manila was issued only for jobs of supreme national importance.

The Whitehall departments concerned were acting rationally, to be sure. Manila hemp comes from the Philippines and had to be paid for in dollars. It occupied precious shipping space over a very long haul by sea, with a screen of U-boats working on the approach routes to British ports. The sisal of East Africa came from within the sterling area and could be imported with much less marine risk. The men of The Gourock nevertheless regretted the falling-off of their traditional standards as imposed from above. Unfortunately, the dilution of quality in the raw materials and the end products was accompanied by a decline of competence in the labour force, also inevitable until the Essential Works Order came into effect.

To take the ropework department as typical—for all other productive departments had their cognate experiences in improvisation with raw materials below the firm's own standards—the call-up of the younger men to the Services meant an increased reliance on female labour and the introduction of older men rather past their best. This labour force was continually changing in numbers and quality, and the normal disciplines of a large manufacturing establishment suffered severely. It was seemingly a little thing, but in fact important, that girls who had done the clerical work in the production departments were gradually transferred to the main office staff to replace young men called up, and their absence from their old posts subtly reduced productive standards and placed on the shoulders of departmental managers still another load of work.

Confusion in the first stages of a lethal war are no doubt inevitable, and the preparations for the defence of the Port Glasgow works seem funny now, though there was no true comedy inherent in a potentially tragic situation. Packed with masses of highly inflammable material, prime source of indispensable war supplies, The Gourock's premises presented a target of perhaps even greater importance than the shipyards. The first defensive step was a great digging of trenches on a piece of vacant ground now covered by the works canteen, and the people of The Gourock went to it with a will. The old hands still chuckle to tell of the young man who, throwing aside his jacket, worked away with pick and shovel and, refusing to stop until dark had fallen, could then not find the jacket, which had been buried under a heap of spoil thrown up by another enthusiast in the next trench.

When the real dangers of bombing got through to the understanding of the authorities the organisation at the Port Glasgow works was geared to meet the threats implicit in the enemy's clever use of incendiaries as providing guiding lights for the bombers. If The Gourock's premises were to go up in flames, then a raiding force would have a guiding beacon that might have been seen a hundred miles away. Thus fifty fire-watchers were on duty every night in and about the rambling buildings, and an eight-man fire brigade was formed and trained. The labour force within the works could not provide a nightly rota of fifty men, and reinforcements had to be brought in from less vulnerable industries in Port Glasgow, notably from the shipyards. During daylight hours over the week-ends the patrols were taken over by girls, leaving the men free for urgent tasks of production and the always harassing job of maintenance. On one Sunday, no doubt bored, one group of those high-spirited creatures had to be disciplined for squirting lemonade from one of the flat roofs on to the heads of passers-by on the road outside.

In due course, the 'phoney' phase of the war passing, the Directors caused a long tunnel to be cut into the hill-side behind the works, and it was certainly one of the largest and safest shelters provided for its workers by any industrial concern in Scotland at least. Over 200 yards long, most of it 45 feet down, under solid rock, it could accommodate 1,000 people. The appointments included a control room, a sick bay, a food store and ample lavatory accommodation; air-conditioning and heating systems were installed. The tunnel was divided into five sections, each with its own separate entrance, each well baffled from the others. There was ample room for all the workers and office staff in the Port Glasgow factory.

While it was needed, however, this superlative shelter gave the men in charge many worries of the social kind. Employees who lived near the works were given passes for their families, and during any hour of alarm the tunnel housed a very strange aggregation of humanity, from day-old babies to nearly helpless ancients. When the alarms sounded strangers sought to gain entrance, and authentic pass-holders had difficulty in fighting their way through the crowds outside the gates. A sort of illicit traffic in passes developed; on one occasion the police had to be called in to handle a crowd nearly out of control. These proceedings were too often diversified by the presence of seafaring men off the many ships at anchor off Greenock, human jetsam of very dangerous seas eager to attract the favours of the mill girls.

The *Luftwaffe* turned its attention seriously on the Tail of the Bank to Port Glasgow area of Clydeside in May 1941, using at once its bases in Norway, the Low Countries and northern France. The heavy raid on Clydebank took place on the moonlit nights of 13th and 14th March 1941. On 5th May a stick of incendiaries came down on the Port Glasgow Works, one to land and burn in a gutter of the weaving shed roof and just below a main look-out station on the flat roof of the yarn store. The outcome is remembered as a comedy in the Keystone tradition. For precisely as a member of the weaving shed squad placed a sandbag on the spluttering bomb the hose on the roof of the yarn

This scene, typical of the severe blitz launched on Greenock, was taken at the corner of Cathcart Street and Duff Street.

163

store came into belated action and drenched him, stifling even the violent language of his protests.

Another episode of the same night was far from funny; it was nearly disastrous. In this case an incendiary bomb pierced the roof of a store, landing neatly in the alley-way between hundreds of tons of manila hemp and sisal in bales. This could have caused a fire that would have been seen many miles away. Fortunately, the firewatchers were immediately on hand with extinguishers and stirrup pumps, and the automatic sprinklers came into action promptly. The domestic fire brigade was also on the scene immediately, but what nobody had foreseen was that the action of water on these raw materials, within a confined space filled with smoke, was to generate the killer gas—carbon monoxide.

Two of the firewatching squad collapsed first. The fireman wielding the hose was the next to be overcome. The present Chairman and Managing Director of The Gourock, Commander H. E. Semple, then took over the hose and had to be dragged out in a state of exhaustion. The direct attack on the fire was at length abandoned. All entrances and exits to and from the building were sealed, and the domestic fire brigade ran a hose along the railway line behind the building and

To safeguard The Gourock's large, varied and vital stocks of raw fibre, shelters such as those shown here were erected in the surrounding district to reduce the risk of loss by enemy action.

164

sought to attack the flames from the roof of the store, while the bands round the bales of hemp and sisal exploded ominously.

There were more casualties before the all clear sounded on the following morning. Three firemen were beaten back in another attempt to re-enter the store. One man, doing his best through a hole in the roof, collapsed and had to be replaced. Finally, in the dawn of a fine May day, the doors of the store were thrown open; the filthy accumulation of water poured out, and the fumes of the poisonous gas went up into an atmosphere already sufficiently thick with the smoke of bombing.

In fact, Port Glasgow escaped the worst of the attack. The *Luftwaffe* concentrated on the larger port of Greenock and caused a great deal of material damage and the loss of many civilian lives. One high explosive bomb came down behind the Port Glasgow works and killed several people in a nearby tenement building. A little later on an unexploded bomb was detected, buried deep in the hillside not far from the laboratory. It was duly detonated, but it is still remembered as a comedy of the period that the explosion took place just when the workers were moving up towards the tunnel shelter. As it turned out, nobody was injured.

Apart from the concentrated attacks during the early summer of 1941 Clydeside enjoyed remarkable freedom from heavy bombing. The *Luftwaffe* found more to occupy it on the Russian front, and the V-weapons of the last months of the war lacked the range to reach so far north. The Essential Works Order had restored a welcome measure of stability to the labour situation; and The Gourock went on producing, and producing, and producing. The demand for ropes and cloth was heavy, and the Services had their special orders to place.

One was for grummets—that is, protective collars for the firing bands of shells. The department set up to meet this need gave work to nearly 100 young girls and, in full production, it could turn out up to 50,000 grummets each week. It is an irony of history that neither the shells nor their collars ever went into action. The former were of a type that neither side in the conflict dared to use, and most of the shells are now where most costly things of the kind should be, at the bottom of the Atlantic.

A stranger but more valuable contribution to the war effort was made by a department mysteriously known as F.E.20. Its business, an odd departure from work in textiles, was to turn out fuse caps for bombs; and the teething troubles inseparable from the installation of metal working in such an environment were numerous and wearing. The plant consisted of high-speed turret lathes, thread milling machines, vertical-drilling machines and the conventional centre lathes. These were manned in double shifts by some 20 operators in each shift, and the Air Ministry installed an inspection unit. This extension of The Gourock's normal activity is known to have made a very useful contribution to our armament as the last of the air battles were building up to the pitch of fury.

Some spectacular orders were given to the ropewalk department, already sufficiently busy with the task of keeping up normal supplies. From time to time the Admiralty required giant ropes, of the finest manila hemp, for such special purposes as deep-sea salvage and the fuelling of warships at sea. These were either of 18 inches, or even 20 inches, in circumference. A coil of the 20-inch ropes weighed three and a half tons. If the seaman found them heavy to handle, the experts in Port Glasgow found them very heavy to splice and difficult to manufacture in every other way. Anybody who has witnessed the process of fuelling at sea—say, of a destroyer by its parent oiler—has seen, one might say *felt*, the fantastic strains put on those Gourock hawsers, especially if the waves are running high. This is a case in which expert seamanship has to be matched by workmanship of the highest quality in the tools the mariner is using.

On the whole, however, The Gourock was fortunate in escaping extreme dislocation through bombing or through shifts in working emphases. If Port Glasgow was almost at the limit of concentrated bombing range in 1941, there were still the branches in areas liable to heavy attack and in the fishing capitals of the East Coast. As it turned out, the total damage in these places was negligible, except in the case of Lowestoft. Aberdeen, Cardiff, Milford Haven and Glasgow—despite the heavy raid on Clydebank—could return clean bills of health, however much daily work might be disturbed by the occasional raider. Fleetwood was a lively place throughout the course of the war, but The Gourock's premises there came by no harm. North Shields was kept busy servicing the convoys that assembled there, but damage to property consisted only of broken windows and slates through the effects of blast.

It is more remarkable that branches in large centres exposed to concentrated as distinct from sporadic attacks were not more sorely hurt. The city of Hull suffered grievously, but The Gourock Ropework Company's branch there, kept busy with the braiding of nets in particular, got off with one blast-damaged door and some shattered fanlights. Here, as elsewhere, the damage much more closely affected the homes of the workers. The firm's premises in Liverpool were close to Exchange Station, the Mersey Tunnel and the Docks; and there were many nights of terror during the attacks on Merseyside—yet only one incendiary bomb, promptly extinguished by the storeman, came dangerously near the building.

Of the branch in Birmingham one could say that it bore a charmed life during the inferno of 1941. On one night business premises on three sides of The Gourock's headquarters were set on fire, but an incendiary bomb that fell in a store full of rope next door had failed to explode! Even in Plymouth, the target of specially violent attacks, one incendiary bomb and some broken windows made up the closing score. It is a domestic joke that the then manager had been away on business in Cornwall and, on his return, was indignant that the *Luftwaffe* had dared to attack The Gourock's premises when he was not there to defend them.

Oddly enough, the memories of those who worked for The Gourock in London during the emergency are tolerably light-hearted. No grave damage, beyond the inevitable delays, was done to stores; and while firewatching was a heavy burden on the male staff at headquarters near Tower Bridge, the young ladies of the London office staff enjoyed a curious *safari*. The then London manager, Mr J. Dykes Hutchison, was an ebullient and generous personality, and during the first days of September 1939 he moved the girls and their office equipment to the comparative safety of the sitting rooms of his house at East Molesey, turning his home into an office. Some of the girls even slept there during the working week, the one in charge of the filing cabinets near to freezing in the garage.

The adventure, so typical of a period now nearly forgotten except by older persons, had the atmosphere of a television comedy, especially when in mid-1940 Mr Hutchison decided to marry again. The young women had to leave East Molesey, premises being found for them farther up the Thames near Hampton Court. These were young women very much on their own. The survivors can laugh about it now, but the situation was quite extraordinary and so typical of the emergency, what with the nightly duties of firewatching and the frequent and prolonged electricity cuts, it is something that the isolated ladies made friends with the local Home Guard and helped to sustain them with viands at all hours of the night.

If we can laugh at some aspects of our war experience, however, it is because we must. As with a thousand other organisations, at no base of The Gourock Ropework Company in the United Kingdom were there many moments free from concern. In particular, the seaports of the East Coast of England were pounded almost daily for years on end. It was nevertheless only in Lowestoft that grave damage was done, when blast from bombing along the main street of the town affected The Gourock's premises in Lancaster Place and a male worker was killed. While the *Luftwaffe's* attack on Clydeside was of short duration, we may tremble to think what might have happened had that fire at Port Glasgow on 5th May 1941 not been held under control.

The Gourock Ropework Company was very lucky in its wartime experience. So was the nation that depended so much on the steady flow of its products.

Henry Bell's 'Comet'—rigged, of course, like so many famous ships before her and since, with Gourock ropes.

Chapter XII

ADVANCE AND ACHIEVEMENT

On an August day in 1812 there sailed down the Clyde from Glasgow to Greenock, the ship channel now quite safe for navigation, a vessel of a stranger type than the harbour had ever seen before. She was quite small, only 43 feet 6 inches overall, but she was propelled by two pairs of side-paddles driven by a steam engine. This piece of machinery, now in the Science Museum in South Kensington, is nearly 5 feet in height, but it could develop only 4 horse-power: less than a modern motor-cycle engine the size of a tea kettle.

The river banks were lined by crowds eager to behold the first passage down the Clyde of this monstrous novelty. Some hoped that the *Comet* would blow up and provide them with an interesting spectacle; many of the older generation honestly believed that she was a monstrosity, defying the divine powers of 'the Almichty's ain wind'. Although hundreds of small boys ran with her along the river banks, jeering and hoping for a sensational crisis, the *Comet* did not blow up. After a passage of some five hours over the course of 20-odd miles, a piper blowing lustily in the bows, she tied up at Greenock's Custom-house Quay. The lines that held her there were provided by The Gourock Ropework Company.

Those who prophesied a catastrophic fate for the *Comet* had not read their history with care. Two steamboats had already plied safely on Scottish waters; notably the *Charlotte Dundas* on the Forth and Clyde Canal. Robert Fulton had already his *Clermont* on a regular and successful run between New York and Albany. We must not, however, underrate the achievement of Henry Bell (otherwise an inn-keeper in Helensburgh) in having the *Comet* built and put into service. She was, in fact, the first steamship used in the Western Hemisphere for reasonably successful purposes of commerce, and as such she figures largely in the tapestry of history. It is of special interest in this history that much of her came out of Port Glasgow.

The wooden hull was built by John Wood on a site in Port Glasgow now properly marked by a plaque set into the wall of the East Yard of the Lithgow shipbuilding concern, and John Wood, a fine boat-builder of the old school, may have had the responsibility of providing the ropes and cordage for the revolutionary ship and gone to his near neighbours up the hill, The Gourock Ropework Company. (One hopes that they were paid for their work. Henry Bell was an attractive and ebullient person, but he had an airy attitude towards his creditors. And it may be noted at this point that the future Mrs John Birkmyre of Broadstone was, in her childhood, one of John Wood's favourites and used to sit with him in his office.) One notes that cordage, as distinct from mooring ropes, must have come into the contract. In suitable winds the *Comet* carried a large squaresail, the tall smoke-stack serving as mast, and the staying of this erection must have required a good deal of material. Since the vessel was no longer than a modern fishing boat of the seine—or ring-net type, however, neither the ropes nor cordage would be of more than moderate weight.

Then, The Gourock, having provided the ropes and cordage for the *Comet* in 1812, were called upon to provide the springs, hawsers and ropes for the *Queen Mary* of 1936-38, 1,019 feet in length against

43 feet 6 inches; 81,000 tons against 25; some 30 knots against 5 with luck.

The comparisons are dramatic in the extreme. They provided the material of a legitimate publicity 'gimmick', and they have so served a generation of newspaper men. One may suggest that the point of greatest importance has been missed, however. To put it crudely, a firm is not asked to provide the ropes for a *Queen Mary* unless its products are known to be of the highest quality. The true interest of the *Comet-Queen Mary* association is therefore that, over the long period of 130-odd years, The Gourock Ropework Company had maintained the highest standards in its products, and that it had maintained a continuity of reputation.

Although a big one, the *Queen Mary* job presented no special problems, and although the ropes supplied for the *Queen Mary* were capable of taking massive strains, they might have come out of stock, for they were of a type supplied to shipping concerns over a long period of years. So, as always, there went into their making the finest manila hemp and the anxious concern of highly skilled craftsmen.

The Gourock produced for the *Queen Mary* an armament, so to call it, of twelve ropes of Hystrain manila weighing together 7½ tons. But the journalists who like to tell the story in the *Comet-Queen Mary* context have apparently not come round to the fact that a similar order was put through in respect of the *Queen Elizabeth*. For that they are hardly to blame, to be sure. The *Queen Elizabeth's* departure from the Clyde was an operation shrouded, and very successfully so, in security precautions. The Gourock had to accept the order in the strictest terms of confidence, and they were given very little time to complete it. The job was done according to schedule, however, and many of the men and women who helped to produce those stout hawsers must have been specially thrilled to see the great ship go down to the sea under the shadow of the tall buildings in which they were produced.

The experienced ropemaker loves a challenge. It has been seen in another chapter that, during the Second World War, the Admiralty required The Gourock Ropework Company to produce some quite monstrous pieces for special purposes. There was a time when The Gourock produced to order—absurd as it may seem and certainly interrupting the flow of normal production—considerable quantities

These special hand-woven rope mats used in the underwater testing of missiles illustrate the many and varied unusual uses to which Gourock ropes are put.

of *flat* ropes. That is, a series of ropes was laid parallel and sewn together; these were required either as buffers for drop-stamp hammers or, in tarred flax cordage, for colliery brake ropes. Paunch mats, rope mantlets, explosion mats—call them what you will—were another sideline the Gourock were called on to produce as a contribution to the war effort in the early forties. These were hung over wall openings in munitions factories to deaden the force of accidental explosions and safeguard adjacent departments in the event of such happenings.

A series of rope strands called 'fexes' were hung over a taut boundary rope and plaited together diagonally until a square or rectangular mat was formed. The number and the length of the fexes depended, of course, on the size of the mat to be made.

In more recent years a number of large mats of an entirely different design and construction have been manufactured as padding for the base of missile testing tanks. These are hand woven with heavy warp and weft ropes and—as may be imagined—are both difficult to construct and awkward to handle.

Quite another sort of task, a real fancy job that challenged the most refined skills of ropemaking, was that of supplying the ropes and running gear for *Mayflower II*.

Readers of a younger generation may have to be reminded of the nature of this project. It was the dream of Mr Warwick Charlton who, during the Second World War, produced the imaginative idea that the people of Britain should subscribe towards the building of an exact replica of the Pilgrim Fathers' ship; this to be sailed across the Atlantic from Plymouth, England, to Plymouth, Massachusetts, and there handed over to the American people as a goodwill gift. Post-war difficulties inevitably delayed the practical launching of the scheme, but it began to take active shape in 1955, when the task of building the hull was entrusted to the old firm of J. W. & A. Upham of Brixham, specialists in wooden shipbuilding. The appointed designer of this second *Mayflower* was Mr W. A. Baker of Hingham, Massachusetts.

Mr Stuart Upham of the building firm elected to have the ropes and running gear made by The Gourock, with which his own firm had been dealing for more than a century. Later on he was to tell the news agencies that 'The Gourock Ropework Company Ltd. are probably the only people in the world capable of producing the ropes to our specification.' These were elaborate in the extreme. It took more than a year of research and consultation to determine with accuracy the rig of a three-masted vessel of the 16th century, then to draw up the necessary schedules. This was, in the absence of ancient records, a nice task of inductive reasoning, and the old records of The Gourock were indispensable. The experts were glad to fall back on that native product, Robert Freeland's essay on the art and science of ropemaking, and indeed its pages yielded up such secrets as how exactly, for example, *Mayflower's* main- and fore-course taper tacks must be made—information not known to exist anywhere else.

As there are different kinds of hemp so do their qualities vary, for instance, First or best quality for strength & wear is the Polish or Riga Rhine.

Second quality	S' Petersburgh Cd Clean
Third	"	S' Petersburgh Clean
Fourth	"	Polish Outshot
Fifth	"	S' Petersburgh Outshot
Sixth	"	Polish Pass

Other kinds of hemp there are such as Manilla which makes excellent towing—lines and running rigging, also Bombay hemp, Italian, American &c but the Russian is generally preferred for marine purposes—

When the hemp is spun into yarn it is then tanned with boiling tar (Not that the tar adds to its strength but only as a protection against wet & rot) and the best tar for this purpose is allowed to be the Archangel, When the process of tarring is accomplished, the yarn should be turned over and allowed to lye in an airy place to cool and harden for a week or two previous to being made into rope—

The Principles of ropemaking are the combination of yarns properly twisted in themselves, and these again twisted into quantities according to the size of the rope required, and in such a way as that each thread will bear its proportion of weight—

As regards size & twist their proportions will be given in the Rules & Tables as set forth in the following treatise, which hope will be found satisfactory and useful as a reference book, and explanatory of this useful Art and Article of manufacture

Rob' Freeland
1857

Robert Freeland, retired master-ropemaker with The Gourock, produced a painstakingly compiled and classically hand-written volume which he presented to the Company. It represents the sum of one man's lifetime of learning and part of the introduction is reproduced here.

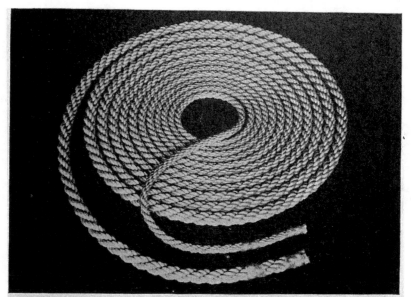

This is ropemaking: 'Mayflower II's' main-course taper tack—a rope tapering evenly throughout its length and extremely difficult to produce—was made possible only from ancient information contained in Robert Freeland's Treatise.

At length, a final conference went over every inch of rope and cordage to be used—its size, construction, lay, function, run, load and so on, and the finalised results were flown over to Mr Baker in the States for his approval. He suggested only a few minor modifications, and the work was at length put in hand.

Skilled men had to return to the arts of ropelaying by hand, and there joined the enthusiasts on the job the late Jimmy Starrett, B.E.M., for 63 years master-ropelayer with The Gourock, delighted to come out of retirement to meet this challenge—involving more than 400 ropes of 28 different sizes and 20 different constructions and lays— challenge to the rare skills still deployed by a commercial concern.

Another ship with her own story in American waters was rigged with The Gourock's finest products: *Sceptre*, the 12-metre yacht that challenged for the *America's Cup* in 1959. This contract involved the production of the yacht's running rigging in Terylene and her mooring ropes in nylon. It was the happy thought of Mr David

'Mayflower II' at sea. Captain Alan Villiers, her Master, was able to report afterwards that, in all the complex rigging, there had not been a single failure or 'hot-spot' throughout the voyage.

Boyd, her designer, that all the ropes involved should, for quick recognition in the excitement of racing, be coloured according to a simple code. For example, the jib halyard-tail in Terylene was blue, the spinnaker halyard yellow, and so on. This rigging had to stand up to hard usage during the grim working-up process firstly in this country, then off the American coasts, and then during the actual races. The *Sceptre* failed to bring the cup back to Britain, but it was certainly not the ropes that had failed. When the yacht was brought back home the ropes were returned to Port Glasgow for examination in the laboratory. They were found to be in first-class condition, some of them scarcely marked, while the colours, so long exposed to salt, air and sun, had faded only slightly.

One of the most romantic of all The Gourock's innumerable associations with fine ships was through the famous *Cutty Sark*, a ship that was in fact not the fastest clipper ever built but one whose strange history and remarkable survival have restored to the British public some sense of the glory of the great days of sail. When she was fitted out at Greenock in 1869 her ropes of soft hemp were provided in the ordinary way of business by The Gourock Ropework Company, and no doubt these were worn out during the 'races' from China with cargoes of tea, during her many years in the Australian wool trade, and certainly during her long spell as a freighter under the Portuguese flag.

It was an inspiration that prompted Captain Wilfred Dowman to save her from the 'knacker's yard' and have her moored in Falmouth Harbour, restored to her original rig and maintained as a sort of national monument. A largely private effort could not, however, keep the old ship in good trim, and when a national campaign in the mid-1950's, warmly supported by H.R.H. the Duke of Edinburgh, ensured her survival in a special berth at Greenwich, The Gourock was again called in to provide the rigging. This time the chosen material was Terylene, resistant to bacteria and acid-laden industrial vapours. The Terylene Polyester Fibre was supplied free of charge by I.C.I.; it was made up at Port Glasgow by The Gourock's craftsmen, also free of charge. More than ten miles of rope went into this labour of love.

The study and development of synthetic fibres in ropemaking, taken up by them in 1938, brought The Gourock in 1960 to create what was almost certainly a record. This was on an order from the Government of Ghana, which required for use as permanent springs in one of its harbours two coils of rope, 12 inches in circumference. Each was of 120 fathoms in length; each weighed approximately 28 cwts. These monsters of Gourock nylon each had an estimated breaking strength of approximately 124 tons. They were the largest synthetic fibre ropes ever made by The Gourock Ropework Company, and they were almost certainly the largest of the kind ever made by anybody at that time.

A little later the Company's experts produced twelve huge 'strops' for very heavy work in the oil industry. These were made up from lengths of Gourock nylon rope, 10 inches in circumference. Thirty feet long, the strops, with a thimble at one end and a loop seized in the other, were mainly covered in heavy flax canvas and represented a very unusual application of the ropemaking skills.

The great and ancient art of ropelaying has its traditions, but these two examples of recent work show how the craftsman, wedding his

'Cutty Sark', surely the loveliest of all the 'tall ships', is re-rigged in Gourock Terylene rope: she stands here in her permanent berth at Greenwich as a proud monument to the greatest days of sail.

ancient skill to relatively new materials, can successfully meet the challenge of modern industry.

The Gourock's enterprise in the matter of net-making has already been discussed, especially with reference to the efficiency and success of the Wing Trawl, but it is well to emphasise the complexity of this fascinating art.

Reference works on fishing methods show in graphic form how, right round our British coasts, the regional fisherman evolved his own netting device to meet local conditions. The variety of these is endless —from the Conway Dredge to the Weston-super-Mare Swing Net, from the Keer Net of Poole to the Shank Net of Southport and the Fyke Net of the Fen Country. But fishing on the large scale to satisfy the abnormal British appetite for fresh fish is largely conducted by three different methods. The first is by the traditional Drift Net, which hangs in the sea like a curtain and, as the name suggests, drifts with tide and wind or is gently towed, the fish of the appropriate sizes being caught by the gills in the meshes. This is the old, traditional method of deep-sea fishing, and it has the economic advantage of sparing the immature fish that can pass through the meshes. The economics of modern life, however, have inspired more deadly techniques.

It is commonly agreed that one of the most lethal devices is the Ring Net, much used in the Firth of Clyde and thence across to Ireland and down to the Isle of Man. The operation is carried out usually by boats in pairs, and very seemly craft they are. Roughly, the method is that when the senior boat has spotted a shoal on the echo-sounder, the sister-ship carries the net at speed in a wide ring round the shoal, returning to tie up with its mate. The lower ends of the net are then drawn in to form a bag, and when this is finally brought to the surface the catch is scooped out with the brailer, another net that, managed by hand, has the shape and dimensions of an outsize jelly-bag.

More commonly used in European waters, perhaps less indiscriminate, is the Seine Net, and the Gourock Wing Trawl, although not of this family, is frequently used as a Seine net, particularly in Scottish waters. The Gourock Ropework Company, it should be understood, cannot easily deal in local specialities; its concern is almost wholly with large-scale manufacture of netting materials, whether that

179

is to be made up for trawling, ring netting or static salmon nets. But the Wing Trawl is a special product worked up by The Gourock's designers, scientists and craftsmen from the Danish original and proved by elaborate tests in many waters, proved by its wide acceptance by the British and Eireann fishing industry. But this in itself is a vast field, great enough in its scope for The Gourock to have now included it in their book* on Deep Sea Trawling—a book already established as a standard work on the subject.

Net-making is big business, as the phrase goes, but it is pleasant to recall a fairly recent occasion on which the resources of The Gourock were enlisted in a picturesque cause at the other end of the scale. Messrs Denny of Dumbarton were to launch the anti-aircraft frigate, H.M.S. *Jaguar*, the christening ceremony to be performed by H.R.H. Princess Alexandra. They apparently foresaw the possibility of slight mishap on an important Royal occasion, and The Gourock was invited to provide a Terylene net of small mesh so that, when the traditional bottle of champagne smashed on the ship's bows, there would be no danger of small pieces of glass bouncing back on to the launching platform. The gadget was duly manufactured, hardly the size of a woman's net shopping bag, and the record is that it discharged its function admirably.

Ropes and nets form the greater part of The Gourock's total output, but a most substantial part is represented by the production of cloth in the various forms that have already been described. Though its managers traded in cloth, probably woven in Port Glasgow, it does not appear that the ropework founded on the shores of Gourock Bay in 1777 produced anything but ropes and cordage, but the original Port Glasgow Rope and Duck Company certainly did. The fact is implicit in the style of the concern, and we have the firm evidence of the first Letter Book that the company was mulcted in considerable quantities of cloth when the armies of Bonnie Prince Charlie passed through Glasgow in 1745.

The lay reader may require to be reminded that 'cloth' in this context does not mean what the word means to the housewife, the tailor or the dressmaker. This cloth is heavy stuff, generally woven from flax or cotton to be made up after proofing into wagon covers, tents, ships' furnishings and so on: protection for heavy goods exposed

* 'Deep Sea Trawling and Wing Trawling'.

to heavy wear and extremities of weather. The importance of these fabrics was emphasised during the course of legal proceedings mentioned in an early chapter—the arbitration proceedings in which David Edward Johnstone sought to secure from the partners of The Gourock Ropework Company on his withdrawal from the firm a larger meed of compensation than they saw fit to offer him. This conflict produced a quite farcical situation.

There was no difficulty in arriving at a fair estimate of the value of the physical assets of the company in the shape of buildings, machinery and stock; it was quite another matter to agree as to the value of that imponderable but important item in the balance sheet, the firm's goodwill. Thus, Johnstone's lawyers produced copious evidence to the effect that Gourock Sailcloth, then sold under the trade mark A1, was undoubtedly a product of the highest quality,

The famous, and first, Trade Mark of The Gourock. It should be noted that the two upper sides of the triangle each have five dashes or strokes: this represents the traditional five stitches per inch demanded of the sailmaker of earlier days in his hand-stitching.

setting a standard throughout the trade. To back this contention the legal men produced an array of ships' captains, merchants from overseas, ship-chandlers—and even trade competitors!—all to declare that Gourock Sailcloth was of uniquely fine quality. So the partners in The Gourock Company were forced into the absurd position of suggesting that their cloth was not so very fine as all that, and their case was ingeniously conceived.

The chief evidence on behalf of The Gourock Ropework Company was given by the then Chairman, Henry Birkmyre II. His argument was that no firm can produce perfection all the time. Mishaps in manufacture were bound to occur, and when that happened it was the fixed policy of the firm to send one of the partners, usually the Chairman's brother, James, to investigate the causes of complaint, even if it had come from the Antipodes. If it was discovered that the fault had originated in the works, then the goods complained of would be replaced without question. In other words, the cunning suggestion was that it was not so much a question of supplying a good article as of giving what would nowadays be called 'service' on the highest level. As we have seen, Mr Johnstone was not awarded the vast sum he no doubt hoped for in the way of compensation.

Gourock Sailcloth, then, was the true ancestor of Birkmyre's Cloth, a prouder appellation and one destined to become even more widely known. (One wonders what the first Henry, the young man from Kilbarchan, would have thought of this romantic distribution of his unusual name!)

It appears that most of the credit for the development of Birkmyre's Cloth should go to James Birkmyre, son of Henry II. It was he who devoted much of his leisure to hunting and point-to-point racing, often stumping about the works on crutches after mishaps in the field, but he was no idle young man of means. It was he who mastered the science of proofing cloth, and that by patient experiment, and he thus made a large contribution to the prosperity of the family business.

It has been shown that The Gourock had some trouble with its patent cloth in the early stages. The process of manufacture involved the use of certain acetates, the cloth immersed in the chemical bath at certain temperatures for certain periods of time, and it was found that in the early stages of experiment the treated material was apt to overheat on drying. The rest was a process of trial and error that led to demonstrable success, confirmed by the demand for Birkmyre's Cloth from all over the world. We may reflect that the Birkmyre brothers were then working without benefit of a laboratory and a trained scientific staff.

Thus, Birkmyre's Cloth is used for a very wide range of goods, large and small. Perhaps its most spectacular application has been in the provision of 'the Big Top', the trade name for a large circus tent.

This is an artifact of much greater complexity than most laymen would, or could, imagine. The spectator at the circus is aware mainly of the dome of canvas above his head and over the ring, and he may concede to himself, above the happy cries of children, that the making of it must have been a tolerably big job. But even if he has gone so far, does he pause to wonder how, in a small world created out of cloth and rope, the animals are ushered on to the scene in exact order; from whence the clowns make their diversionary entrances; how all sorts of

The current 'four-poler' Big Top of Bertram Mills' Circus. To the average person a 'Big Top' is just a large tent: to the manufacturer it is a nightmarish complex of canvas, rope, steel wire rope, hide and special fittings, all most cunningly co-ordinated.

animals, mutually antipathetic—horses, sea lions, chimpanzees, elephants and the rest—can be introduced without conflict?

In short, the production of a Big Top is much more than a mere job of manufacture. It is to a large extent an architectural achievement, with fine work in the drawing office required beforehand as in the case of, say, the production of a ship. Those who pass through the main entrance and pay their shillings at the cash desk see the ring and the orchestra in its enclosure; they cannot naturally see the corridor-like compartments behind, in which the performers and animals are marshalled in order of appearance with military precision. This movable creation in cloth is, in a sense, as complex in its layout as any cathedral.

A large amount of material, as well as careful craftsmanship, go to the making of a Big Top. In all, it uses up some 4,500 square yards of cloth in eight separate sections. When stepped up on its masts, two or four, it is on the average 210 feet in diameter, the height from the level of the ring to the apex of the dome being 55 feet. The total weight is in the neighbourhood of four tons. But the cloth and the masts must be heavily reinforced, for such an expanse of canvas could too easily rip or collapse in a high wind. The walls of the marquee are therefore strengthened at every ten or fifteen feet of their height with interlacings of rope. Finally, the interlocking system of guys, webbing and steel-wire rope reinforcement is of astonishing complexity. And yet the circus owner must carry all this material about from stance to stance, set it up and take it down again perhaps at the end of just a few days—a feat of logistics that should fill us with admiration for the industry and skill of the showmen, for the experienced design and workmanship of the manufacturers: a thought all the more impressive when one thinks of the large number of human beings under any Big Top at any performance.

So The Gourock has sent out on to the highways of the world many of these outsize temples of delight, many of them gaily woven in striped cloth according to the circus master's fancy. Port Glasgow has provided large-scale jobs for all the leaders in the business of showmanship—Bertram Mills, Smart, Chipperfield and the rest. From that smallish Clydeside town, with hardly enough flat ground about it to accommodate a Big Top in full fig; from the descendants of men who first learned their craft in sailmaking, there have gone all over the globe many of those great canvas marquees in which so many generations have found delight.

The Gourock Airhouse, introduced in the United Kingdom in 1959, is the old-fashioned marquee perfected and mechanised, as it were, but made possible by the creation of very strong, lightweight impermeable cloth woven of synthetic fibre and P.V.C.-coated. Of a handsome oval shape, it is inflated with air at low pressure, introduced through ducts by fans working from small motors outside the fabric. Naturally, the problem of sealing such an erection was a difficult one, but it was solved by the provision of air-sealing doorways and by care in methods of consruction and erection; and it is remarkable what small quantities of air are required to keep it inflated and what heavy loads can be suspended from the roof without serious deflection.

The total effect is pleasing in that, apart from the shapeliness of the external features, the Airhouse has no poles to break a vista and is completely protected within from the weather. It is thus a ready made, portable home for exhibitions, conferences and the like, and as such

Almost like a visitor from outer space this giant Airhouse—believed to be the largest ever built in Britain—was given a test-erection near Port Glasgow, as seen here, before being sent out to Nairobi for the Kenya Maize Marketing Authority for whom it was specially made. This Airhouse, 240 feet long, 60 feet wide and 30 feet high, has a volume of almost one-third of a million cubic feet and will be used in Kenya for the storage of bagged maize. The whole nylon envelope is P.V.C. coated in green and special conveyor doors are provided at each end for handling the bags of maize in and out.

it has been used. One Gourock Airhouse accommodated the Mid-summer Ball of a Clyde yacht club, and it served the purpose admirably —even if some young sparks created a brief deflationary diversion by slipping the fan belts off the pulleys. During 1960 a London con-structional company used a Gourock Airhouse to facilitate their work on an open building site and enjoyed such complete protection from extremities of weather that they completed in three months a job that would otherwise have taken six, and at a substantial saving in cost.

This indication of the shape of things to come sprang from a British brain, that of Dr F. W. Lanchester. From 1910 onwards various attempts were made on the other side of the Atlantic to get the scheme working, but with indifferent success. More recently, The Gourock Ropework Company's Canadian subsidiary, Gourock-Bridport Ltd., of Montreal, made substantial progress as did certain American concerns, but the Gourock Airhouse of today is mainly a product of the ancestral works in Port Glasgow. Into producing this shapely artifact in lightweight P.V.C.-coated nylon cloth went the patient, and, over a long period, devoted work of scientists, draughts-men and sailmakers in a concern dating from 1736! That seems a thought of some importance in terms of economic history.

Chapter XIII

LINE OF SUCCESSION

These two pictures have a remarkable and industrially-unique link: Henry I, Henry Birkmyre of Kilbarchan (left), is the great, great, great, great grandfather of Hugh Notley Semple (right), himself grandson of the present Chairman and Managing Director.

As soon as work ceased at noon on Saturday, 23rd May 1936, some 2,000 employees in the Port Glasgow, Greenock and Govan factories of The Gourock Ropework Company hurried home to prepare themselves for an outing in celebration of the firm's bicentenary. Coloured streamers flickering from the carriage windows, they were carried in special trains to Gourock Pier—and one notes the symbolism of this destination—and boarded the two crack turbine steamers of the then L.M.S. Railway, dressed over all with bunting and flags. So, in the early afternoon, a large, gay and perhaps occasionally noisy party set off on a cruise down the Firth of Clyde.

The route chosen is one of great beauty. Those children of the crowded places, most of them excited girls, may have paused to stare at the peaks of Arran as the ships carried them up the outer arm of the Kyles of Bute to Tighnabruaich and then, after a brief halt there, up the Firth again and into the fjord that is called Loch Long. It is doubtful if many of that happy party had much of an eye for scenery that day, however, they were having a lovely trip at the bosses' expense, and, reading a fading newspaper report of the junketings—concert parties, beauty competitions, community singing and the rest—one fancies that the youngsters were more interested in their paper hats and the plenty of good things they got to eat and drink.

They were all home about nine o'clock in the evening as recorded on the grandfather clock the senior managers had presented to the Directors on the evening before: a handsome timepiece that decorates

Part of the start from Gourock Pier of The Gourock's Bicentenary Cruise, 1936.

what is still invariably known as the Back Office, never the Board Room, though that is what it is in effect. And one wonders how many among those two thousand people realised that they were in fact themselves historical figures. They could have looked back from Gourock Pier and seen the point at which the long ropewalk of the original Gourock Ropework Company ran down to the shore. As the fast turbine ships carried them down the Firth they could have reflected that it was in these very waters, in their millions, there used to swim the herrings that set up the demand for The Gourock's wares. They could have seen in the deep-sea shipping passing up and down the users of their own products in rope and cloth.

Probably none did, for they were mostly young and female, properly determined to have a good time. It remains true that these girls were historical figures in the private pageantry of an ancient industrial concern. Many of them could say that their mothers, their grand-mothers, even their great-grandmothers, had worked at The Gourock's looms before them. It is not utterly fanciful to imagine that there may have been among the two thousand on holiday that day one or two descendants of the men who wove the cloth exacted from the Port Glasgow Rope and Duck Company by Prince Charles's Quarter-master-General when the Jacobite army passed through Glasgow in 1745.

In the Directors' party on this cruise there were seven Birkmyres in the direct line of succession along with some absorbed by marriage into that enduring dynasty. It is a singular fact that few of the Birkmyre males, through four or five generations, lived to any great age; most of them achieved the three score of the allotted span, but not the extra ten. It is all the more remarkable that so many Birkmyres were on hand to join their workers on the occasion of the bicentenary cruise 144 years after the founder of the Port Glasgow line, Henry Birkmyre I, came to work in that small Clydeside town in 1792. With Birkmyres still at the head of The Gourock Ropework Company and its subsidiaries we have a family record stretching over 168 years, taking 1960 as our deadline.

It seems desirable at this final stage of our journey through time to rehearse briefly the sequence of events.

The first of the Birkmyres, Henry, was born at Lochwinnoch in 1762, went from Kilbarchan to Port Glasgow as foreman with the Port Glasgow Rope and Duck Company in 1792 and, in 1814, was assumed a partner in The Gourock Ropework Company that had taken over from the older firm. The Rope and Duck Company had been founded in 1736, The Gourock in 1777.

It is perhaps well to remember that the first Henry Birkmyre had married his full cousin, Agnes Birkmyre of Kilbarchan, she being nearly a year older than he. They died within a few years of each other during the 1840's, leaving five children. Of these only one, William, born in 1802, figures in the story of The Gourock Ropework Company, but most prominently so.

A curious entry on an inner flyleaf of his own family Bible suggests that this William was carefully prepared for his future responsibilities. He went to Glasgow as a boy of 14, presumably to gain experience with some merchant there. Still barely 19 years of age, he sailed for America and worked in the States for three years, and the assumption must be that he was making contacts, in the modern phrase, and no doubt improving The Gourock's large trade on the other side of the Atlantic. He returned to Glasgow in 1823 and, a year later, came under his father's wing again in Port Glasgow. In 1827 he went into the mill—as he describes it in his own handwriting—becoming in effect Works Manager when the faithful Archibald Baine and the first Henry Birkmyre passed from the scene within a few months of each other.

189

It has already been shown that this William Birkmyre of the second generation could fairly be called the constructive genius of the business. He was responsible for vastly improving the techniques of manufacture; the Company's turnover was greatly increased during his term of office. It is more to the point here that his authority within the firm greatly strengthened the position of the Birkmyres as against the influence of partners who had mostly inherited their stock. It would be a proper reading of economic history that William Birkmyre firmly laid the foundations of the family's ultimate control of the business.

This first William was just short of 60 when he died but, as we have seen, he left a family of six, of whom five were sons. Of these sons, forming a third generation, three were most actively engaged in the business.

They were Henry II, John and Adam. The last was a delightful eccentric but also a successful traveller all over the world in The Gourock's interests. John seems to have been the quiet one, his social activities much under the control of an able wife who was also something of a feminist, but he was as a rock of steadiness at the side of his older, abler brother, Henry II. His portrait shows the latter to have been a portly man in the Victorian mould with a rufous beard. (John's was black.) He was very much the master, the progressive one. It has already been told how, with his brother-in-law, R. G. Somerville, he acquired the mills at New Lanark and in due course added their manufacturing power to that of The Gourock, the firm's first major extension outside the Port Glasgow–Greenock area.

It was with this generation of Birkmyres that there came at once an emergence of individuality and close association with the public affairs of Port Glasgow. (As we have noted, one of the brothers, William II, after a spell in India, took little or no part in the affairs of the Company, opted for a political career and became Member of Parliament for the Ayr Burghs. He remained faithful to his native town, however, and in 1895 bought a stretch of ground high on the hillside near Glenhuntly House. This he had laid out as a public park and presented it to the community. It is still the Birkmyre Park.) We know that William I was progressive in business, but we have no clue as to the personality of the man. The obituary notices duly record that he was a worthy citizen; Provost of Port Glasgow and a pillar of the United Secession kirk the family attended, but the quiddity of the man is lost under the blanket of flat prose produced by the square yard in the provincial newspapers of Victoria's days. But his sons—Henry, John and Adam—come up as 'characters', lively figures at least in oral legends of quite recent provenance. In 1955, at least, there were still old people about the mill who could remember them clearly.

It is also notable that the lives of the three effective brothers neatly spanned the same period during their working lives—roughly, between 1850 and 1900. There were less than two years between Henry II and John, born in 1832 and 1834 respectively. Adam, the youngest of the family, was a latecomer, born in 1848. They all died during the first decade of this 20th century, at the fatal Birkmyre age of about 60— three of the brothers, including the M.P. for the Ayr Burghs and Rev. Archie, the minister—within one year. Adam ended his diverting life in Switzerland in 1906; John of Broadstone outlived them all until the age of 75, but he had by that time long withdrawn from active participation in the business.

Thus the three brothers who had come into control of The Gourock Ropework Company rode high on the tides of an expanding economy, applying their brisk talents to the improvement of their commercial situation and the expansion over the world of their influence as acknowledged manufacturers of first-class goods. But The Gourock remained in its character a family business; at no time did one of its partners loll in ease in sunny climes. As we have seen, they built their houses on the outskirts of Port Glasgow, and it was an article of family faith that they owed duties to that community.

The church affiliations of the earlier Birkmyres form an interesting subject of study. William I, son of the original Henry, was prominently involved in the great affair of the 1843 Disruption, when the Church of Scotland was split wide open on issues of patronage and 487 ministers 'walked out', surrendering manses and stipends in a unique demonstration of democratic feeling. One of these was the Rev. James Morison, minister of the Newark Chapel-of-Ease in Port Glasgow, and most of his congregation elected to follow him. Prominent among them was William Birkmyre I, and by that time he was Provost of Port Glasgow, so that his example had a great deal of local significance.

The dispossessed congregation sought at first to worship in the graveyard of the kirk, in the open air, but they were shortly evicted from that windy stance and were forced to wander extensively round the town in search of accommodation. For a period, for Communion gatherings, William Birkmyre I gave those supporters of what was now the Free Church of Scotland the use of The Gourock Ropework Company's 'Dock-side Store' in the main street of the town. For these services cordage and other gear were piled at one end of the loft and covered with tarpaulins; the small office at one end of the shed became the Vestry for the Sacrament.

This congregation ultimately acquired, with the help of a legacy, a place of its own and a manse for the incumbent. Having returned, like so many others of the original congregations-in-revolt, to the broad bosom of the Church of Scotland, it is now the Hamilton Church, Port Glasgow, the name deriving from that of the local merchant whose testamentary dispositions helped it to find a permanent home. William Birkmyre I remained, under the minister, the leader of this religious group, and the kirk records show that many men of The Gourock's staff have been among the office-bearers over a long period. It is more interesting that of this William's sons, Henry II broke away to build his red sandstone church at Clune Park, probably on one of the small denominational issues that could in those days too easily create bitter schisms. It is perhaps more interesting that his brother, John of Broadstone, remained a pillar of the Hamilton Church all his days. He superintended the Mission Sabbath School for 48 years on end; it is on record that he conducted family prayers at Broadstone until the eve of his death. The organ still used in the church was the gift of Mrs John Birkmyre.

The ecclesiastical proceedings of Henry II and Adam Birkmyre were of a stormier nature. The Scots have always been (or perhaps one should say, used to be) fervent and contentious in matters of Church politics as well as in the rituals of worship, and Henry II fell foul of his associates in the Free church the family had supported for a hundred years. A masterful man, he financed the building of a breakaway kirk, and it is there to this day; a quite agreeable building in red sandstone on the main road, only a few hundred yards east of the mill. The congregation is now, after the period of schisms and reunions that afflicted the Scottish kirks for many years on end, safe in the bosom of the national Church as Clune Park, a parish church within the Church of Scotland.

One irreverent anecdote associated with this place of worship and the Birkmyre brothers is still cherished by their descendants. It appears that the choir was recruited mainly from among the workers in the mill and trained by a foreman with musical tastes. One evening the choristers were enjoying a break from practice when word came through to the hall that one of the great men was approaching. The conductor urged his flock to their feet with a cry, 'Here's the boss coming,' adding desperately in the idiom of working hours, 'Sing, you b——rs, sing!'

That tale is matched by the authentic record of a characteristic outburst by that lively citizen, Adam Birkmyre. He was concerned at one time to make a gift to the parish church of St James in Kilmacolm, and he suggested a peal of bells for the steeple. Chiming bells were probably regarded by the minister and Kirk Session of those days as having dangerously Catholic associations, and it was communicated to Adam that they would prefer to have one single bell in the Presbyterian tradition. 'Very well!', cried the frustrated donor. 'They'll have the loudest bloody bell in Kilmacolm.' And so it is to this day.

John Birkmyre does not appear to have been capable of such flights of eccentricity, but the gift that he and his wife made to Port Glasgow on the occasion of their golden wedding was substantial and perhaps more necessary in a small burgh before the National Health Service and improving transport facilities widened the areas of hospital responsibility.

The Broadstone Jubilee Hospital, opened in 1907, of what used to be called the 'Cottage' type, stands high on the hill above the central area of Port Glasgow. It boasts 30 beds and, while declining the care of maternity cases, deals briskly with industrial accidents, apt to be frequent in a shipbuilding region, and with urgent surgical cases. To the first conception John Birkmyre and his wife contributed a Trust Fund of some magnitude, to which many people of means in Port Glasgow added generously, but that, and the intimate direction of the hospital, have passed under the somewhat impersonal care of the Scottish Western Region Hospitals Board.

This benefaction might be described as the last public act of the third generation of Birkmyres in their relationship with Port Glasgow. Members of the fourth generation active in the business were already running into the era of high taxation and heavy Death Duties. This fourth generation consisted entirely of the children of Henry II, for John of Broadstone was childless and Adam a bachelor. Henry II's family was a large one, twelve in all, but half of them were women, and some of the men among them chose the life of leisure.

Typical of a more leisurely era now gone, the local Artillery Band plays in front of Broadstone House, Port Glasgow house of John Birkmyre I.

The family was beginning to thin out, in fact. One of the daughters, Agnes, married William Lithgow of the shipbuilding firm of Russell and Company; his name survives in the title of that powerful shipbuilding and engineering consortium, the Lithgow Group. One of the sons—another Henry but hardly entitled to a dynastic number—came to rest at length in Honolulu, where he strangely acquired some sort of reputation as an amateur meteorologist. The youngest brother, Archibald, as we have already seen, was sent to India, prospered and was eventually created a baronet.

In the direct line of management at Port Glasgow, however, the effective men after the death or retirement of Henry II and John I were two of the former's sons, James and John II. It was this James who, by dint of patient research and experiment, gave The Gourock its invaluable asset, Birkmyre's Cloth. Though younger, John II was perhaps a more masterful personality, an able man of dark colouring, and he was soon enough to be left with almost sole responsibility for the control of the Company's affairs, including the onerous task of winding up the large estate of his Uncle John of Broadstone. These two brothers held the fort through the first three decades of the 20th century, but

James died a bachelor, and of John II's four children only two were boys, both fated to early deaths.

There thus loomed up what can perhaps be described as a crisis in the Birkmyre succession to the business. John II was himself ageing as 1930 approached. He had already lost his older son, Henry III, in 1928 and at the age of only 36, an eager, progressive and imaginative young man. His younger son, John III, had to take over the reins of management at an early age: a somewhat lonely figure in this parade. Over a scene essentially tragic in the family sense, there were gathering in the United States the clouds of the Depression that hit the British economy so savagely in 1931.

Burdened with sorrow and anxiety, John Birkmyre II looked about him for ways and means of securing the family succession within The Gourock. Already his own younger son, John III, had had to accept the responsibilities of Chairman and Managing Director, the father fit only to advise, and there was no other male Birkmyre of age in sight. In the meantime, however, Jean, John II's older daughter, had married Lieutenant-Commander H. E. Semple, R.N., who had seen violent active service in the First World War and was by his training and experience of handling men a suitable candidate for managerial responsibility. Mr Semple was finally persuaded to resign his commission and join the Board, learning the business with the quickness of a man still young and well taught and well protected by the Old Faithfuls of the permanent staff.

But this was, so to speak, only the end of one act in a domestic drama. In 1942 Mr Semple's brother-in-law, John III, died before he had reached his 40th year. So heavy was the shock, the father, John II, survived only a month or so thereafter. The direct male line was not thereby extinguished, however, Henry III had left a son, John Fullarton Birkmyre, but he was still being trained, and H. E. Semple, as the man on the spot, was left with many heavy burdens to bear. Those of us who live in an age of amalgamations and take-overs may profit by observing the tenacity of the Birkmyre clan in clinging to its traditions and accepting the responsibilities that go with tradition.

The situation created by the crisis of 1928–29 was eased in due course. The bank suggested the appointment of a Director with specialised financial ability and recommended the election of Mr Andrew MacHarg, head of a leading firm of Chartered Accountants in Glasgow and an authority on most aspects of Scottish industry. In this case, however, Mr MacHarg (later Sir Andrew) suggested that he should have the help of an expert in the trade, with the result that Mr Alexander Brander Allan joined the Board in 1930. A. B. Allan had been active as a principal in the wire rope business for many years; and his special knowledge, backed by Sir Andrew MacHarg's financial acumen, steadied the boat through the depression and fortified Mr H. E. Semple's grasp of the huge business.

One of The Gourock's distinguished ambassadors at large was John Kerr of whom it would not be an exaggeration to say that the Company's present extensive organisation overseas has been built on the foundation which he laid. Most of the half century of his working life with the Company was spent on the export trade and even after he had been elected a director in 1911 he continued to travel very extensively, expanding the Company's business into new markets and establishing overseas agencies. He died in harness in December 1942 at a Board Meeting.

Mr Allan was not by any means a young man when he became a Director of The Gourock, but there was never one more lively. He travelled extensively abroad and did much in the way of the reorganisation of branches overseas. One of his pet interests was the manufacture of wire rope, and it was he who urged his fellow-Directors to acquire the Archibald Thomson, Black & Co. concern at Shettleston. He was Chairman of The Gourock from 1942 to 1945. He lived to the great age of 96, always interested in the affairs of the Company. Indeed, he outlived by a few months Sir Andrew MacHarg, who had died in August 1959.

The combined influence of these two able men saw The Gourock through the difficult period that had inevitably followed the deaths of three male Birkmyres in quick succession. It gave Mr H. E. Semple time to find his feet in a strange environment and to master the intricacies of a complex commercial structure; it gave the young men of the future time to grow up and then come in to learn the business, as the phrase goes. John Fullarton Birkmyre—only son of Henry III and invariably known as 'Mr Ian'—had come of age in the mid 1930's. His younger cousin, Henry Birkmyre Semple, son of Jean Birkmyre, followed him in the learner's part. In the meantime Mrs Semple, Jean Birkmyre, served for a few years as an Executive Director.

Jean Birkmyre—Mrs H. E. Semple.

Here was a woman of high personal charm who might be said to have had the word 'Gourock' written on her heart. Practically the last survivor of the older generation in the direct line, she was properly proud of the achievements of the Birkmyres, and she could express her pride with vigour as occasion required. Her grasp of the Company's affairs was sound, her business sense acute; and then she could contribute her meed of good looks and warm charm to the success of her husband's world travels on behalf of the firm. She liked to say towards the end—as can her husband—that she knew personally every member of The Gourock's staffs overseas. Jean Birkmyre took her place in public affairs, in the social, political and cultural activities of Renfrewshire in particular, but The Gourock and its affairs were nearest her heart.

Mrs Semple was given little time to enjoy her position as Executive Director. Intermittent illness plagued her last years. She bought for herself a modest place on the Argyllshire coast, where she had spent so much of a happy childhood, and there she died on 15th March 1959. She had the satisfaction of knowing that the affairs of The Gourock were again safely in Birkmyre hands—her husband, her nephew and her only son in command. It should be said here that the writing of this History was one thing she had long wanted to see accomplished. Indeed she amassed a wealth of material and made at least a tentative beginning on the narrative proper. Most of the personal anecdotes and legends concerning members of the Birkmyre family came out of her abundant stores of family memory.

As we know, The Gourock Ropework Company, having existed as a purely private partnership for more than 160 years, was incorporated in Scotland—but as a Private Company, limited by shares—on 21st October 1903. On 24th October 1940 it was converted into a Public Company. During the early months of 1960 formal application was made to the Committee of the Glasgow Stock Exchange for permission to deal in the whole of the stock and therefore to have the values of the shares quoted in the Exchange lists and in the public prints. The statutory advertisement of this step provides us with a useful check on the state of affairs in the year that has been chosen as the deadline for the completion of this History.

The Authorised Share Capital is £1,260,000, made up of 360,000 five per cent Cumulative Preference Shares of £1 each and 3,600,000 Ordinary Shares of 5s. each. The Directors are listed as Hugh Egerton

Semple, Chairman and Managing Director; John Fullarton Birkmyre, Sales Director and Deputy Chairman; David Lumsden Morgan, Works Director; Henry Birkmyre Semple, Works Director, and John Maxwell, Writer to the Signet in Edinburgh. Mr Maxwell is the legal representative of family trusts, and he has no executive functions.

Mr Morgan has come right through the mill, almost literally, since he joined The Gourock in 1921. In due course his specialty became that of costing, a science delicately balanced as between statistical acumen and an exact knowledge of manufacturing processes. Since the death of John Birkmyre III in 1942 Mr Morgan, whatever formal title he may have been given within the organisation, has been the Company's chief adviser in methods of production and technique, working closely with the Chief Chemist. He is recognised throughout the trade as a supreme authority on his subjects and has held high office in the organisations of the Hard Fibre industry.

It is of interest that the home addresses of the three Directors in the Birkmyre line are all in Kilmacolm, Renfrewshire, in the upland village turned by old Adam into a sort of Birkmyre colony. Kilmacolm is only some four or five miles from Port Glasgow by road, a short journey in a modern car. Mr Morgan lives in Greenock, still nearer the Works. Thus the decision of authority on the highest level is always at hand, no matter how far a young Director may be travelling in search of business. It is a rare thing nowadays, considering the amount of capital involved, but The Gourock remains a family business, the Directors in daily attendance, meeting for their elevenses in the old Back Office, a good coal fire lighting the portraits of the Founding Fathers.

It is always surprising that this firm, its name borrowed from another town on the Firth of Clyde, six miles away, should be so much a part of Port Glasgow. We have seen how various members of the Birkmyre family acknowledged their responsibility to the community by the gift of a hospital and a church notably, then in instances innumerable by financial support of good works in the locality. When Port Glasgow Town Council was at its wit's end to find space for houses under the steep foothills, The Gourock Ropework Company handed over its own range of workers' houses for a nominal sum that was but a tithe of the site value. The Company gave the municipality the use of water from its own upper reservoir at Dougliehill, saving the community a huge sum in capital outlay, but not without some physical embarrassment to itself.

Port Glasgow cemetery lies to the east of the town, covering an irregular stretch of hillside. Its western gate is hard by the house called Springbank that Henry Birkmyre II built for himself. Both house and burial ground have been surrounded by the domestic building of the new age, but it is quiet up there on the slope, elevated above the surging traffic of the main road by the shore. There stand within rings of turf the monuments to at least three generations of Birkmyres who lived and worked in Port Glasgow over a century of time.

The graves are marked by two simple obelisks in grey granite, unadorned save for names and dates. One memorialises the great third generation, the sons of William I—Henry II and John, along with their M.P. brother, William. The other, about a hundred yards away, records the misfortunes of John II when, towards the end of his own life in late 1942, he lost his two sons while they were still in their thirties.

The obelisks stand on a distinct ridge of the irregular cemetery grounds. They look out to the sea, not far above the point at which the ship channel of the Clyde merges with the deep water of the Firth—that channel and estuary on which the fortunes of The Gourock Ropework Company and the Birkmyres were essentially based. The graves of famous shipbuilders surround theirs, each name starting a story in the mind of every wayfarer who understands something of the regional circumstances. Those descendants of old Henry Birkmyre from Kilbarchan lie in the goodly company of their peers in the van of industrial progress.

And the line of succession is secure in the persons of Alan Henry, son of John Fullarton Birkmyre, and Hugh Notley Semple, son of Henry Birkmyre Semple—both schoolboys as this history goes to press, both heirs to the great tradition it has sought to expound.

Alan Henry Birkmyre

Hugh Notley Semple

DATE DUE / DATE DE RETOUR

CARR McLEAN   38-297

CPSIA information can be obtained
at www.ICGtesting.com
Printed in the USA
BVHW050316070223
658034BV00003B/61